MW00851283

The INCREDIBLE
Work of the
ELEMENTARY
SCHOOL

THIRD EDITION
Martin J. Wasserberg
Bradford L. Walker

University of North Carolina—Wilmington

Kendall Hunt
publishing company

Cover images © Shutterstock, Inc.

Kendall Hunt
publishing company

www.kendallhunt.com
Send all inquiries to:
4050 Westmark Drive
Dubuque, IA 52004-1840

Copyright © 2011, 2013, 2019 by Bradford L. Walker and Martin J. Wasserberg

ISBN 978-1-5249-8975-0

Printed in the United States of America
10 9 8 7 6 5 4 3 2 1

CONTENTS

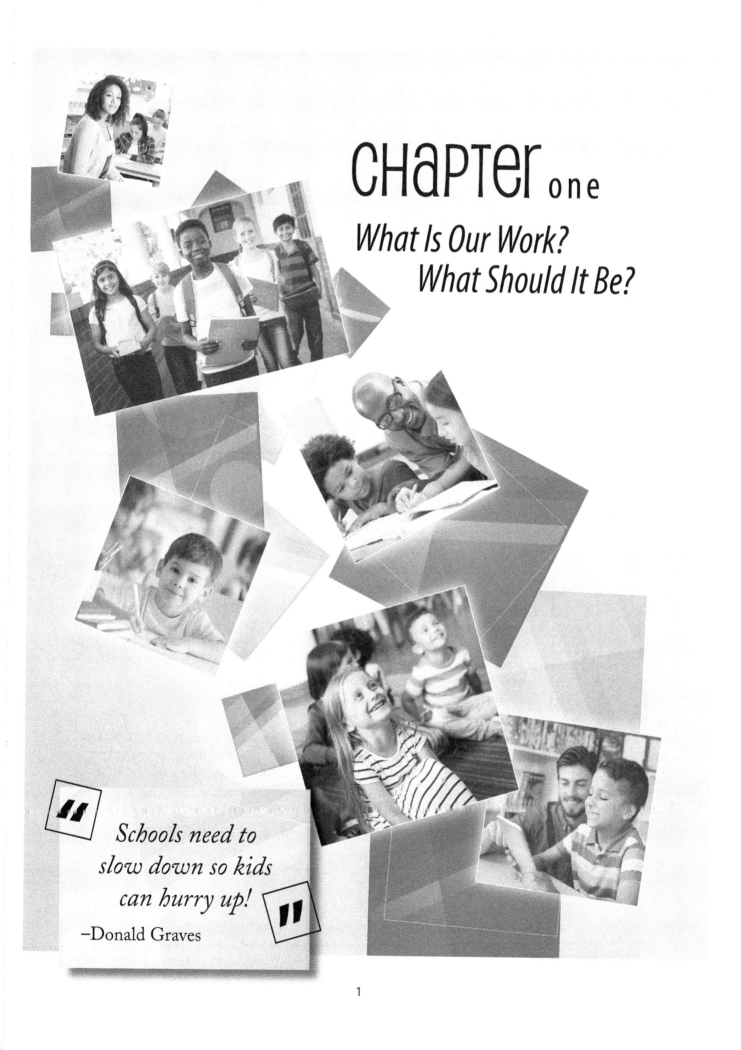

CHAPTER one

What Is Our Work?
What Should It Be?

> " Schools need to
> slow down so kids
> can hurry up! "
> –Donald Graves

Opportunity *for* dialogue:

What do you think Donald Graves means by this statement? Can you see evidence that schools are moving so fast that kids aren't able to learn? Can you identify specific situations in which schools are so busy doing that kids don't have the time to learn? Can you identify situations in which schools have slowed down so learning can happen more effectively? Has this happened in your experience?

The incredible work of the elementary school is something that is talked about in many circles. Certainly, legislators and other government officials talk about our schools and how effective they are. Many politicians feel obligated to help move the work of our schools forward. Business leaders are concerned about the work of schools and the impact that schools might have on their ability to hire competent employees as well as attract top people from around the nation and the world. Naturally, they want to build their businesses in areas where there is a good supply of qualified workers. Parents and other family members are concerned about the schools their children go to. They want to ensure that their students are getting the best education possible—that they are prepared in every way possible for success in life. Parents send their most precious possessions, their children, to school, knowing that these children will spend a huge part of their early lives at the school, in the care of teachers.

Additionally, educators are concerned about the effectiveness of schools. Teachers come into the profession because they want to make a difference in the lives of their students and their families. Teachers are about helping students learn. They want to help students expand their vision; to see the possibilities of what their lives can be. Teachers work to help students gain all of the skills necessary for success in life and to be good, honest, contributing members of society. Teachers love learning and they work to help their students become life-long learners as well.

Opportunity *for* dialogue:

What other stakeholders can you identify? Why are they interested in the work of the schools and the success of the schools? What impact does this have on our work?

With so many stakeholders concerned about our work, it seems only natural that there are many plans for exacting accountability. Most of these plans look at test scores and other objectives that can be easily measured and analyzed. Even when more holistic evaluation instruments are used, the results are often reduced to a score so that comparisons can be made and stakeholders can look at numbers to determine how schools are doing with their work. As well-meaning as many of these programs might be, it appears that many, if not all, of them have missed the mark. They have significantly impacted the work of the elementary school to be sure. The focus in schools has quickly shifted to the test scores and preparing children to pass the tests.

The impact is further illustrated by research suggesting that teachers do not enjoy their work as much as they did before. Children, as well, have been described as not enjoying school. The pressure placed on teachers and students to perform is taking its toll.

> Dr. Katie Schlichting, a professor at UNCW, asked her students if they thought children were happy in school. They replied, "Of course!" She gave them an assignment to specifically look at the children in their assigned field experience school and return to class next week ready to report. The students were amazed to realize that many students were not happy and did not enjoy school.

Other questions that might be asked are:
- What happened to recesses?
- What happened to field trips?
- What happened to time to talk with students and for students to talk with each other?
- What happened to the fun in school?
- What happened to spring festivals, winter carnivals, plays, and assemblies?
- What happened to inquiry and exploring our questions about the world?
- What happened to authentic learning?
- What happened to time to learn, not just go through the motions?

Opportunity *for* dialogue: Do you agree that there is more pressure being placed on teachers and students? Do you think that school children today are not as happy as school children of yesterday?

Another factor that impacts the work of the elementary school, is that schools are simply not the same as they used to be. We often hear people say things like, "Wow, schools are sure different from when I went to school." Others might say,

"That isn't the way we did it when I went to school." "I didn't learn that until Jr. High School." We would probably all agree that schools are different than they used to be years ago. These differences are both positive and negative. Increased access to better and more powerful technology has increased access to information and ways of communicating that were not dreamed of years ago. The Internet, Facebook, podcasts, iPod touches, iPads, texting, tweeting, and much more have created an environment where knowledge is more accessible, and communication can be quicker and more effective. Schools are now better able to focus on every child, endeavoring to ensure that every child is successful and is able to grow in all ways possible. Knowledge about nutrition has resulted in more nutritious meals. A better understanding of diversity has allowed us to help our students come to understand and value the rich diversity that is part of our lives. New knowledge is created every day, adding to the excitement we feel about learning.

On the other hand, some of the changes schools have seen through the years has focused our attention to other areas and has resulted in negative impacts on students and their families. Technology has helped with learning and communicating but it has also isolated us, as more and more people spend time surfing the net and not engaging in conversation with significant others in their lives. A focus on accountability has, in some cases, limited the curriculum as schools have focused on the subjects that are tested—using every possible minute to prepare students to pass the tests. Some teachers have commented that teaching is no longer fun. Many children don't seem to be happy in school. All participants in the school are feeling much more stress and pressure. Things clearly have changed.

Our society has changed dramatically as well. Editorials in newspapers and magazines talk about the selfishness of our country and the inability to carry on civil discourse. It seems we are quick to argue, quick to find fault, quick to place blame on others, quick to want revenge, and quick to exact revenge if we have been wronged. We seem quicker to question authority, to migrate to extremes, and to explain things in absolutes. These changes appear to have created an environment in which authority is questioned, blame is shifted to others, and respect for authority, for teachers, and even for learning is lessened. Much of what schools can offer and what an education can provide are taken for granted.

With the multitude of challenges we face, many decide they will not pursue a career in education. Others lament the difficulties faced by educators and students. Alfie Kohn, a well-known educator and writer, listed the challenges we face. Then he made the statement that all of these challenges and opportunities are the reason we all should be going into education. We need the best in our schools. Our children all deserve excellent teachers and administrators.

With the current situation, it seems natural that if we were to ask a group of people what they thought the work of the elementary school is or should be, we would, likewise, receive a variety of answers. Some possible answers might be, to ensure that every child learns what they should learn; to make sure that children pass the tests; to meet Adequate Yearly Progress; to obtain passing scores on the end-of-grade tests; to learn to read, write, and calculate; and to get ready for the next grade. Still others might suggest that schools should help children learn, prepare for life, learn to function in society, learn to be a good citizen, become a life-long learner,

What Is Our Work? What Should It Be?

5

and prepare for a successful career. Still others might include preparation for life by helping students become contributing members of society, solid citizens, have the characteristics and attributes we value such as honesty, a good work ethic, and the ability to get along with others. Others would suggest growth in confidence and abilities to be successful in all aspects of life. Others would mention that we must help our students come to understand, value, and appreciate the rich diversity that is all around us in our lives and at school—we should help students be able to effectively interact with everyone.

Opportunity *for* **dialogue:** What would you say is the work of the elementary school? Take a minute and jot down a couple of bullet statements that represent your thoughts about what elementary schools should be about.

We would like to suggest that our work in elementary schools encompasses most of the above. Helping students have the skills necessary to pass end-of-grade tests is important. Helping all students meet adequate yearly progress must be a part of our work to be sure. There is so much work to be done and it is so incredibly important. If we do our work effectively, our students will have what they need to be successful in the rest of their school ventures as well as in life. Our work must include preparing our students with the knowledge, skills, and dispositions required by the 21st Century. Our work as teachers is too important to let it be reduced to simply preparing for the end-of-grade test. Our work is vital to each child, to our communities, to our nation, and to the world. Can you see why?

We aren't just teaching students to be able to do math. We aren't just teaching students to be able to read. We are preparing our students to be able to be successful in life—to live life to the fullest extent possible. We are preparing our students to be contributing citizens, effective parents, to help solve the problems of the world, to make our world better because of having lived in it.

This is why the work of the elementary school is so incredibly important. We are the educators in the system that have the first opportunity to help our students grow to be what they will need to be for success in their lives. We are the first ones with the huge responsibility to ensure that all students can learn, will want to learn, and will learn and continue learning.

At the elementary school, we can, and we must, be successful in helping to build:
- confidence
- willingness to take risks
- an excitement for learning
- enthusiasm for using the tools of learning
- safety
- optimism

- abilities to get along with others
- appreciation of and value for the rich diversity that is part of our lives

We could very well ask questions such as, "If our students score high on the end-of-grade tests and reach all of their goals but can't get along in society, have we been successful with our work?" We might wonder, "If our students did not score well on the end-of-grade tests but have confidence in their abilities, are able to work well with others, and are good problem solvers; have we been successful with our work?" "Will we allow the outcomes that can be measured quickly and easily, to become the focus of our work, or will we continue to focus on all aspects of a child's development?"

As we think about the work of the elementary school, a couple of stories might help us.

Mrs. Hannah Gage, the Chair of the University of North Carolina Board of Governors made a presentation to the Board of Trustees of the University of North Carolina Wilmington. In her presentation, she worried that we were putting too much attention on the things that matter least and, perhaps, overlooking those things that might matter most. She said that ensuring that the average SAT scores of our students are higher than other universities or that the high school grade point averages of our students continue to rise, is not the most important thing to consider. She suggested that ensuring that all students graduate or that all students learn, would be a much more important aspect of our work. Her comments apply to all levels of education.

In the movie, *Dead Poet's Society*, the new English teacher, Mr. Keating, tries to help his students take charge of their learning and "seize the day." He encourages them to not let the typical assignments and assessments that often accompany the learning we do in school, get in the way of their learning. He suggests that they go beyond the assignments, be in charge of their learning. As they seem to question the need to study poetry, he tells them, "We read and write poetry because we are members of the human race and the human race is filled with passion. Medicine, law, business, engineering; these are noble pursuits necessary to sustain life. But poetry, beauty, romance, love; these are what we stay alive for."

He then reads Walt Whitman's poem, "Oh Me! Oh Life!"

Oh Me! Oh Life!

O me! O life! of the questions of these recurring,

Of the endless trains of the faithless, of cities fill'd with the foolish,

Of myself forever reproaching myself, (for who more foolish than I, and who more faithless?)

Of eyes that vainly crave the light, of the objects mean, of the struggle ever renew'd,

Of the poor results of all, of the plodding and sordid crowds I see around me,

Of the empty and useless years of the rest, with the rest me intertwined,

The question, O me! so sad, recurring--What good amid these, O me, O life?

Answer.

That you are here--that life exists and identity,

That the powerful play goes on, and you may contribute a verse.

Walt Whitman

Source: Oh Me! Oh Life! by Walt Whitman, 1855.

He sees his work as helping his students gain a voice, learn to think for themselves, be in charge of their learning, and to truly "contribute a verse" to the powerful play of our lives together. Perhaps this is the way to articulate our work in the elementary school. However we look at it, there is more to our work than simply teaching the three Rs. There is more than simply preparing our students for the tests. There is more than satisfying the demands of accountability, regardless of how high stakes they might be.

Dr. Richard Allington (1994), suggests that we have begun to confuse certain aspects of our work. His list of confusions follows. The last two items on this list are the authors'.

- **Teaching vs. Assigning**—do we find ourselves simply assigning work and confuse it with the actual teaching that can so much more fully support learning?
- **Books vs. Blanks**—do we confuse reading real books and having meaningful conversations about them with simply asking students to do worksheets? Do we confuse learning through hands-on activities and meaningful engagements with simply assigning worksheets for students to complete?
- **Experience vs. Ability**—do we look at students and suggest that they have lesser ability when, in reality, they simply have less experience?
- **Acceleration vs. Slowing it down**—do we sometimes think that presenting less and more simplistic material, and doing it at a slower pace, is better for learning than accelerating and challenging all students? Do we keep students from participating in certain learning engagements because we think they can't handle it?

- **Sorting vs. Supporting**—do we think we are done supporting the learning of our students when all we have done is sort them into different groups?
- **Curriculum vs. Instruction**—have we confused our focus so that we spend the most part of our day on the curriculum as opposed to the instruction we provide?
- **Understanding vs. Remembering**—do we measure success because students can remember certain facts, or do we look to measure understanding of those concepts?
- **Letting literacy work its magic vs. Pacing guides**—do we worry more about where we are on the pacing guide, or getting kids into meaningful learning engagements and providing the time necessary for learning to happen? Do we truly believe that learning in and of itself is empowering?
- **Students vs. Learners**—Are we helping to produce students who are good at doing what we assign or are we helping to produce students who are learners in the truest sense of the word?

Source: The Reading Teacher, Vol. 48, No. 1 (Sept 1994) by Richard L. Allington. Copyright © 1994 by the International Reading Association.

Opportunity *for* dialogue:

Can you identify other confusions that might inhibit the incredible work in which we are engaged? What might we be able to do to ensure we are on top of any confusion that might arise?

As we continue to try to articulate the incredible work of the elementary school, it can be beneficial to look at other countries and other cultures as we attempt to articulate what the work of the elementary schools should be. For example, Watson School of Education students have visited schools in South Africa, Belize, and Japan. The information cited here, from students visiting Japan and from Japanese educators visiting North Carolina, seems to be compatible with observations by students visiting schools in other countries as well.

From Japanese educators:
- In America, it seems that you see your task as taming children. In Japan, we see our task as nurturing children.
- Why do students go from place to place in a straight line behind the teacher?
- A high school principal was asked what Japanese educators do to screen students from going to undesirable sites on the Internet. His candid response was, "We don't put the screen on the computer, we attempt to put the screen on the heart of the child."
- When our students learned that Japanese schools don't retain or hold students back because of low achievement, they asked a principal what she would do if they noticed a school at which achievement was lower than expected. Very matter-of-factly, she replied, "We'd probably hire more teachers to help."
- Other Japanese teachers remarked, "We look to America as the center for democracy. However, when we look at your schools, we don't see democracy at

work. Where do students have the chance to practice and learn the principles of democracy?"

From UNCW students:

- Japanese teachers seem to structure less but control more.
- It is amazing how much more they do with music and art in their schools.
- Japanese students are not supervised on the playground at recess.
- I am impressed with the Japanese teachers' belief in the innate goodness of children.
- There is a pervading atmosphere of trust and respect in their schools. They trust their students.
- Japanese students are so happy.
- Everyone shares responsibility for education in Japan. Parents, teachers, students, the government, and many more, all realize the importance of a good education. In the U.S., it seems that everyone is always passing the blame.
- I realize now that the meaning of responsibility goes way past our typical classroom jobs.
- I discovered what I must teach my own students. Hopefully, I can help them understand our American need for forgiveness.
- I learned that technology doesn't drive education—passion does.

A very common observation of our students is that children in other countries seem to have a deeper understanding of the value of education. They seem to know what education will do for them. They are excited to be able to go to school. They are happy to learn. Schools in many, many countries are able to successfully do their work with such fewer resources than we have in America. Our students interning in Belize schools report how shocked they were to realize that they would have to teach in classrooms that did not have computers, that did not have access to the Internet, that did not have much, if any, materials, and that did not have electricity all of the time. They returned much more resourceful, creative, and confident that they can do their work effectively.

Opportunity *for* dialogue: What do the perspectives from other countries add to our articulation of our work?

Lastly, we would like to suggest some premises upon which we base our work and our interaction with students, families, and other educators.

Basic premises:

- More than tests—we are preparing students for life. We are helping them navigate life's issues as they learn confidence, and develop desire, knowledge, skills, and dispositions.
- Children want to learn, are excited to learn

- Children are naturally capable, competent learners
- Children learn by doing
- Children are children
- Children deserve to go home each day excited about returning to school the next day
- Children deserve to be trusted and respected
- Children are why our schools exist
- Children are anxious to be engaged in meaningful, purposeful learning
- Children deserve to be safe and protected
- Children deserve ownership
- Children deserve champions who believe in them and will do what it takes to help them
- Every child deserves excellent teachers
- Children's work is play—it is how they learn about the world and how they grow
- Everyone's answer makes sense to them
- Schools are fun and exciting places for everyone

Opportunity *for* **dialogue:** What would you add to this list of premises? What is important to you? What will you do as an elementary teacher? How might you describe the incredible work of the elementary school?

What Is Our Work? What Should It Be?

11

ELEMENTARY PROGRAMS AND PRACTICES
EDN 300
OPPORTUNITY FOR DIALOGUE

Name:

Chapter:

CHAPTER two

Philosophical Foundations

> "The scandal of education is that every time you teach something, you deprive the child of the pleasure and benefit of discovery.

–Seymour Papert

Opportunity *for* dialogue:

What did Seymour Papert mean by this statement? How might it impact the way you will organize and run your classroom?

The following is a note I received from one of my fifth grade students. We had a message board in our classroom. Students were free to write notes to each other and place them on the message board. I decided that this would be a wonderful way to interact with my students so I made plans to write a note to each student each week.

> EsKLanTag
>
> Dear, mr.walker. the school year is going Fun. I Like it. John Alex and chip said Hi. I relly Like Being in your, class. But can you have me set in anuther chear. Becuse I and kristing took to much, and kive .Plesy. I'm not geting my wroch Done. I'm geting Prett good at spilling . Oont you thick? : your a good teacher. well I got to go By By writh Back

From Literacy for Diverse Learners: Finding Common Ground in Today's Classrooms *edited by Barbara Honchell and Melissa Schulz. Copyright © 2002 by Christopher-Gordon Publishers, Inc. Reprinted by permission.*

Opportunity *for* dialogue:

What can you tell about Angie from the note? If you received this note from Angie, how would you respond? My note back to her was a quick, "Hi Angie, thanks for your note. Please tell your brothers hello for me. I agree. You are getting better at spelling. I can see it, too. Keep up the good work. Thanks."

Later that year, Angie came to me and said she wanted to write a story about her grandfather. I told her that I would be very excited to read her story. She then went back to her table and started talking with her friends. I inched closer to the table to hear what they were discussing. She was saying, "If you were going to interview your grandfather to write a story about him, what questions would you ask? They helped Angie write a very good list of questions. She went to visit her grandfather that weekend and came back to school ready to start her story. It went something like this: "My Grandpa is a neat guy and I'm going to tell you about him. When he was in fifth grade he was the best marble player in the school. If he was late getting home he would get whipped with a willow and he had to chop firewood in the dark." About that same time, we had gone to the library and Angie had checked out the book, *The Bronze Bow* by Elizabeth George Speare. It is a wonderful book, a Newbery Award winner. It begins as shown.

The Bronze Bow
By Elizabeth George Speare

A boy stood on the path of the mountain overlooking the sea. He was a tall boy, with little trace of youth in his lean, hard body. At eighteen Daniel bar Jamin was unmistakably a Galilean, with the bold features of his countrymen, the sun-browned skin, and the brilliant dark eyes that could light with fierce patriotism and blacken with swift anger. A proud race, the Galileans, violent and restless, unreconciled that Palestine was a conquered nation, refusing to acknowledge as their lord the Emperor Tiberius in far-off Rome.

Looking down into the valley, the boy could see the silver-gray terraces of olive trees splashed with burgeoning thickets of oleander. He remembered that in the brown, mud-roofed town every clump of earth, every cranny in a stone wall, would have burst into springtime flower. Remembering, he scowled up against the hot noonday sun.

This book was a challenge for Angie. At one point during her reading of the book she explained, "This is a hard book but I think I'm getting the gist of it." I think you will be able to see that she was. After a few days writing on her story, Angie came back to class stating that she had a new way to start her story. She had started it as shown:

One in a Million

A boy stood on the mountain path. He was tall and handsome with blonde hair and eyes as blue as the summer sky. His name was George. George Brailsford. But as a little boy, he was called Leonard. The mountain path was a special place for Leonard because it led to his Uncle Hazel's ranch up Hobble Creek canyon. On the side of the trail it had a wicked, rushing river. On the other side of the trail were big boulders. Leonard lived in Springville in a small cabin in the east area. He thought to himself, "I'd better be getting home." He began to walk, dragging a stick behind him leaving a line in the dirt trail. He had to hurry because if he was late he would get whipped with a willow and if he played late he would have to chop firewood in the dark.

***They got help from the doctor once again, and Leonard recovered and went up on the mountain path, but now he was a man.

Opportunity *for* dialogue:

What evidence do you see in this story of my philosophy? How did my philosophy impact what I did in the classroom and what the students were able to do? Can you see why knowing our philosophy can help us become more effective teachers?

A philosophy is a set of beliefs, a set of assumptions, that guide our actions. Our beliefs about how children learn and how to best support that learning will impact our work. Our philosophy will determine:

- the kind of classroom we create
- the kinds of engagements into which we invite our students
- the way we interact with our students
- the way we come to know them as learners
- what we choose to call success
- how we choose to find success,
- how we assess; what we assess
- how we deal with parents
- the roles we play
- what we do in the classroom
- the places in which we position ourselves
- the time we allocate for learning

Dr. Barrett J. Mandel (1978) has suggested that "…it has always been and will always be who the teacher is, more than what the teacher does, that truly counts." A teacher's philosophy helps to determine who he/she is. Mandel continues, "…a teacher teaching makes choices constantly, selects materials, emphasizes certain values, creates goals, and develops programs. The more consciously the teacher makes these choices, the more likely the students will be assisted along their paths."

It is important for teachers to be able to understand their own philosophy and be able to articulate it along with the consequences for teaching and learning that accompany that philosophy. Clearly, we can find exceptional teachers operating from any of the philosophies. It is our contention that learning is enhanced as teachers are able to understand their set of assumptions and consistently work from that identified perspective, as they help support the learning of their students.

Opportunity *for* dialogue:

Can you articulate your philosophy? What is your set of assumptions about teaching and learning that will guide your work?

While there are many different philosophies at work in the elementary school, for this class we will look at two—behaviorism and constructivism.

Constructivism is a philosophy that suggests that we learn best by doing; especially when that doing is meaningful and purposeful. It suggests that learning happens best when students are engaged in the whole process, not in isolated bits and pieces of the whole process. Inquiry is looked upon as a most powerful learning strategy. A constructivist philosophy suggests that teachers empower students as learners, help them find their own voices, and help them take ownership in order to help make the learning more meaningful for students. Believing that students learn to read by reading, teachers provide an environment in which there are many, many texts and opportunities to read for a variety of purposes. As they observe children reading, teachers take time to demonstrate other strategies that might help them in the process of learning. If there is a specific skill they would like to teach, they would teach it in the context of real, relevant text. There is not a hierarchy of skills. Children make the connections that they are ready to make. Children interact with the world, creating their own connections to what they already know. Students are encouraged to ask their own questions and seek the answers to those questions. Dialogue is encouraged and students are encouraged to engage in learning conversations, not parroting learned concepts back to the class. Students are encouraged to articulate their own connections, share them with their peers, and receive feedback and ideas about how other students are making sense of the world. Teachers are less concerned with what the students should learn from a specific engagement and are more concerned with watching the student to see what they are doing and learning.

In the science classroom, teachers would be more likely to have students actually do an experiment and then make connections explaining why certain things happened the way they did, rather than have students learn the concepts of science and then do the experiment as a way to demonstrating the concepts learned. In the social studies content, constructivist teachers would create learning engagements in which students could explore the past, answering their questions about what happened and making connections about what it might mean for us in the present. Constructivism suggests that learning happens best as students are empowered as inquirers, following their wonderings of the world. Teachers, then, become facilitators and co-learners with their students, ensuring that demonstrations are available and that students have access to the engagements that will be most supportive of their learning.

Behaviorism is a philosophy that suggests that children mature and progress in predictable ways, and that learning should be presented in smaller chunks according to the developmental stage of the learner. Behaviorism suggests that learning is a change in behavior as a result of a person's response to stimuli. It suggests that instruction is carefully broken down into small, successive steps that are carefully designed to maximize the likelihood of student success and to minimize the likelihood of student frustration or failure. Learning can best be supported when the specific concepts are organized in a logical manner, when teachers learn the best stimuli to use to support learning, and when the instruction is organized, precise, and focused. Learning of more complex skills can best happen when a series of smaller component skills are mastered. This philosophy requires a no-nonsense, dedicated learning time that leads to mastery of a skill. Mastery is rewarded. There is a sense of accomplishment as students meet benchmark goals and as skills are mastered. Terms such as mastery learning, programmed instruction, and hierarchy of skills relate to a behaviorist philosophy of learning. If the teacher can gain and maintain student attention, explain the concept in the right way, and help the student progress through the hierarchy of skills, learning will be achieved. A behaviorist might suggest that learning to read cannot be accomplished without first learning the letters and their sounds. The curriculum would then be organized to work through the letters and their sounds in an appropriate sequence—moving from easier concepts to more complex concepts, with the appropriate reinforcement for good behavior (learning) until the letters were learned to mastery. Students would be taught the concept, using the precise methods outlined, then asked to respond to the question showing they know the concept. Concepts are practiced until mastery is obtained. Right answers are reinforced, wrong answers are retaught. In a behaviorist philosophy, there is a time to teach, a time to practice, and a time to apply. Learning is best supported when these times are kept separate and distinct. Reading for real purposes comes later, after the critical skills have been mastered. In the science room, specific concepts would be broken down into essential sub-concepts that would be learned through repetition and appropriate reinforcement until mastered. Then, and only then, the more complex concepts could be learned. Behaviorism would suggest that the specific product is the most important aspect of the learning engagement.

Perhaps it might be helpful to look at these two philosophies from another viewpoint as well. In the math classroom, a behaviorist philosophy would suggest that there is a hierarchy of skills essential to learning math. A student can't possible learn how to divide until he/she has mastered multiplication and subtraction. The program of study would teach students how to subtract and then to multiply and then to divide. Typically, the most important aspect to look at is the answer to the problem. If the child gets the right answers, he/she probably understands the concepts.

In a constructivist classroom, on the other hand, teachers believe that engagement in mathematics for authentic purposes is the best way to learn. Students would be given manipulatives and given tasks that might help them create connections relating to the processes of multiplying and dividing. Students would begin to understand the process of division and why it works. They would come to know the relationships between multiplication and division. They would create their own connections about the relationships between numbers and how division looks in various situations. These connections would be shared with others. Along the way, the teacher would ensure that they understand the process, not just the calculations. The goal is to understand why division works.

Constructivism values:	Behaviorism values:
Process	Product, mastery of skills
Kid-watching	Assessment of skills learned
Learning and inquiry	Focused, directed learning
Learning with students	Teaching the students
Collaboration	Focus to the teacher
Finding our voice	Respond as directed

Opportunity *for* dialogue:

Do you agree with the elements of the table above? What other descriptors would you add to our list?

THE AUTHORING CYCLE

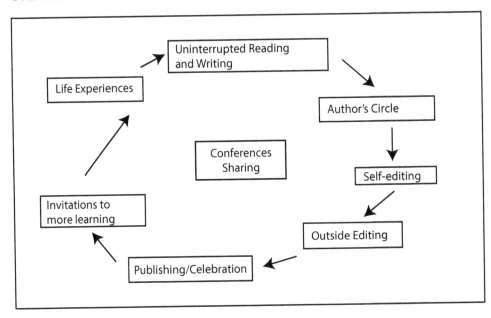

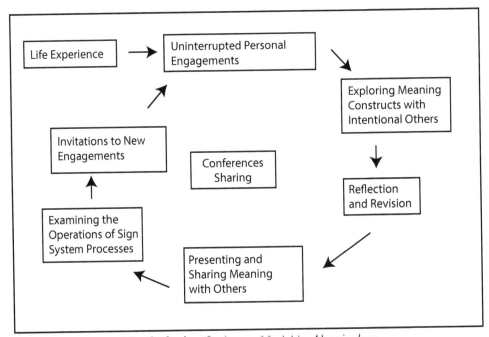

The Authoring Cycle as a Model for Curriculum
Source: *Creating Classrooms for Authors and Inquirers*, Second Edition by Kathy G. Short and Jerome C. Harste with Carolyn Burke.

Opportunity *for* dialogue:

Carolyn Burke created the above authoring cycle to illustrate a structure that would support children in their writing. Can you identify which philosophical perspective it is coming from? Carolyn Burke and Kathy Short then extended the authoring cycle so that it became a model for all curriculum and teaching. The two models stem from the same philosophical perspective. What evidence can you see to support your answer?

Another way to understand the constructivist philosophy of learning is to look at the work of Brian Cambourne (1988). Cambourne was an elementary teacher in Australia. He was shocked by the difficulty his students had as they learned to read. He wondered about this. He knew that the very children who were struggling with learning to read, could speak and listen effectively. They could say what they wanted to say and they understood what others were saying to them. He began to study the conditions that made it possible for children to learn to speak so effectively, thinking that, perhaps, those same conditions might be effective in helping children learn to read.

As Cambourne studied infants learning to speak, he identified seven conditions of learning that seemed to be in place in most situations in which children learned to speak. Those conditions are:

- **Immersion**—children learned to speak because they were surrounded with an almost limitless access to language being spoken. They heard everyone around them speaking and they could see the meaningful context in which that language was used. They could use language or try to use language anytime they wanted.
- **Demonstration**—everywhere they looked, they saw significant people in their lives using language.
- **Expectation**—we all expect young children to learn to speak. It happens so naturally, we don't really think about it. We just know it will happen.
- **Responsibility**—children have the responsibility to determine where they would focus their attention. They could look at the person talking to them and listen to the sounds they were making or they could focus on someone else in the room. They also had the responsibility to make their own connections. We might think they were learning something, but they were focused on something else.
- **Use**—they learned to speak because they spoke. They learned by doing. Usually, children at home don't have structured speaking practice. They get enough experience by speaking. There is not a hierarchy of words to know or strategies to learn. We just communicate.
- **Approximation**—approximations are accepted and valued. Children aren't marked down or punished for the mistakes they make as they learn to speak. The cute, "I wuv you, Mommy," is usually responded to with an "I wuv you,

too." A statement of "We goed to the store," is usually responded in conversation such as, "Yes, we went to the store this morning, didn't we. We bought some milk and bread." Children are encouraged to try, without worrying about mistakes.

- **Response**—the attempts to speak by children are followed with the kind of feedback that allows children to make significant connections about the process of speaking. They often get more feedback than they expected.

Cambourne's Conditions for Learning

Brian Cambourne's Term	Brad Walker's Term	My Term
Immersion	Opportunities	
Demonstration	Demonstration	
Expectation	Trust	
Responsibility	Ownership	
Use	Doing	
Approximation	Miscues	
Response	Collaboration	

Source: The Whole Story: Natural Learning and the Acquisition of Literacy in the Classroom by Brian Cambourne.

Opportunity *for* **dialogue:**　Select your own term for each of Cambourne's Conditions for Learning. For each of the conditions, list two evidences that would suggest that these conditions are part of a classroom and are being utilized to support children in their learning.

We have talked about how these conditions apply to learning to read and write. Pick another content area such as math, social studies, or science and explain how they might work to help children learn in those disciplines as well.

Based on what you know about these two philosophies, try to fill in the chart with descriptions that help us see the difference between them.

Category	Constructivist View	Behaviorist View
Role of teacher	Co-learner; facilitator	Knowledge dispenser; director
Engagements	Process-oriented; authentic	Practice sheets focused to specific skills
Curricular Decisions	• Based on needs of students • Teachers and students make together • A look at the whole process • Meaningful, authentic	• Based on scope and sequence • Teacher makes; program makes • A look at simple component parts • Time to teach and time to practice skills are separated
Success	• Little things that happen along the way; find it where it happens • Process/strategies/depth of engagements	• Pacing guides • End-of-grade tests • Chapter tests • Progress on simple component parts
How to Assess	• Kid-watching • Watch the child in the process of doing the tasks • Qualitative data—description of the process, identification of strategies used, examples of comments made and connection created; analysis of mistakes made to determine the thinking of the student	• Tests • Quantitative data—numbers, scores, number of words read in a minute, number of mistakes made while reading, scores on math tests, end of grade tests
What to Assess	• Understanding of process • Use of strategies • Comments indicating connections being made • Mistakes as windows into the mind of the learner	• Grade level • Proficiency on small, isolated parts of the whole, • Performance on tests and quizzes
Use of Time	• Take time needed for learning to happen • Slow down so kids can hurry up • Take advantage of learning opportunities as they arise	• Time on task • Consistency with pacing guide

Interactions with kids	• Learn together • Let go • Empower • Learner to Learner	• Direct, teach • Teacher to Student • Control
Classroom Management	• Create environment of caring • Help students learn about classmates • Help students understand how to operate in the environment of the classroom and school • Help students take ownership and responsibility of their choices	• Control behavior of students • Rewards and consequences

Over the years, there have been many educational movements that have been tried and discarded. In the 1970s, one of these movements was the open school or the open classroom. This was a physical arrangement of the school that created classrooms without walls. The open walls facilitated the work of teachers—they could easily organize groups of students for learning that would facilitate their interests, match their abilities, and use the effectiveness of team teaching. What many schools failed to realize, however, was that this was also a philosophical change. Many schools could sense the value of this movement, but were not given the time to really understand the philosophical foundations upon which it was built.

During the training sessions, educators were shown examples of how this would work with students in their classrooms. When the teachers implemented the ideas, everything was fine until they faced a situation not covered in the training. Without the understanding of the philosophical foundation of the movement, they were left to make decisions on their own, without the support of this deep understanding. Many of the decisions made were inconsistent with the philosophical foundation, the theory behind open classrooms. When these decisions didn't work, educators quickly jumped to the conclusion that this was another program that wouldn't work, and they discarded it for something else—usually what they were doing before.

I actually did my internship in an open school. I was assigned to sixth grade. There were three sixth grade classrooms with three teachers. There were no walls between the three classrooms. Curtains could be pulled if classrooms needed to be alone. Without walls, students could move freely as they went to the different groups to which they had been assigned for various subjects. The teachers also could move to points from which they could be most helpful to students. Sometimes, all 90 students would meet together for instruction. Much team-teaching was utilized. While this was an innovative approach to learning; to me, it was chaos. The students in one classroom seemed to be distracted easily by the students in another classroom. The noise level was too high for my tastes. It was a difficult internship to say the least. I did learn much from the students and from my partnership teachers, but it was a difficult time for me.

Upon graduation, I began interviewing for jobs. During one interview, I learned that the school was an open school. When the principal offered me a job, I told him that I had interned at an open school in another county and that I didn't want to teach in an open school. He said that they had planned to have a closed classroom in each grade in order to provide a choice for parents. He offered me the fourth grade closed classroom and I accepted. I was working out of state at the time and went back to my other job. A few weeks before school was to start, I moved to this new city. I went in to speak with the principal and he informed me that none of the parents had wanted their children in a self-contained classroom at any grade level. He then took me to my corner of the big room, which housed three other classrooms. I could see all of them and they could see me since there were no walls. I was horrified but there was nothing to do since it was too late to look for another job. I jumped in with both feet, even though I was very anxious. To my surprise, I found a totally different situation than the school at which I had interned. Here, the faculty understood the theory and the philosophical foundations of an open school. Once I understood the philosophy undergirding the practice, I was prepared to make decisions consistent with the philosophy when the need came. I learned that this is a very powerful way to support learning. In fact, I came to realize that the open school was consistent with my own philosophy about teaching and learning. It was fun and exciting for students as well as teachers.

Opportunity *for* dialogue:

What made the difference? Can you identify other situations in the work of the elementary school where philosophy has had a distinct impact?

ELEMENTARY PROGRAMS AND PRACTICES
EDN 300
CAMBOURNE'S CONDITIONS OF LEARNING

Name:

Opportunity *for* dialogue:

Select your own term for each of Cambourne's Conditions for Learning. For each of the conditions, list two evidences that would suggest that these conditions are part of a classroom and are being utilized to support children in their learning.

Cambourne's Conditions for Learning

Brian Cambourne's Term	Brad Walker's Term	My Term
Immersion	Opportunities	Evidences:
Demonstration	Demonstration	Evidences:
Expectation	Trust	Evidences:
Responsibility	Ownership	Evidences:
Use	Doing	Evidences.
Approximation	Miscues	Evidences:
Response	Collaboration	Evidences:

ELEMENTARY PROGRAMS AND PRACTICES
EDN 300
OPPORTUNITY FOR DIALOGUE

Name:

Chapter:

CHAPTER three
International Perspectives

"
Education is life,
not preparation
for life.
"
—John Dewey

Opportunity *for* dialogue:

What did John Dewey mean by this comment? Do you agree with him? Do you see evidence in elementary schools that would suggest they agree with Dewey? Do you see evidence in elementary schools that would suggest they disagree with Dewey?

In our attempt to understand the incredible work of the elementary school and to prepare ourselves to do that work, there is much we can learn from other cultures. As teachers and students travel to other countries or interact with different cultures, it can be very generative to see how these students and teachers deal with some of the same issues with which we grapple. For example, watching a 5th grade teacher in another country use strategies for classroom management can help us examine our own beliefs and practices, and identify ways to be more effective. Discussing specific techniques in planning for instruction can help us identify ways to be more effective as we plan for learning. Sharing our own philosophical perspective on teaching and learning enables us to discuss consequences of the beliefs that we hold.

In this chapter we will explore examples of experiences in the elementary schools of Japan. We will then identify some principles about learning and teaching that might hold implications for what we do in our classrooms. We will then finish with a discussion on those implications and how they might be made manifest in our classrooms.

UNCW students who travel to other countries to observe in their schools report fantastic learning experiences in those countries. Students usually report that teachers in other countries often do much more with much less. Class sizes are often much higher than we experience in the United States. Access to the Internet and other technology is often limited. As students travel to Japan, they are often surprised at the lack of technology in their schools. Most schools have computer rooms but students and teachers do not have access to computers, SMART Boards, or the Internet in most of their classrooms. In Belize, students were amazed to learn that even having electricity is something that cannot always be counted on. Many schools in other countries do not have central heating or central air conditioning. And yet, these schools seem to be able to accomplish so much in helping their students achieve in school and in preparing to be successful in life. Comparisons of student achievement show that many of these countries do as well or better than we do.

Another common report is that school children are so very happy and that there seems to be a stronger commitment to school than is often shown in America. Our students report that school children in these other countries seem to have a deep understanding of what schools and learning can do for them. There is a higher level of respect for schools, teachers, and administrators.

Our students often come back with increased confidence in their abilities to be creative, to make decisions on the fly, so to speak, and to plan for effective learning without the resources we are so used to in our country.

It is important to understand that culture has a definite impact on schools. It is not meaningful to simply compare what we do with other countries without also looking at the cultures involved. Some things we are able to do, they could not do, and vice versa.

Opportunity *for* **dialogue:**

Why do you think students in other countries might have a deeper understanding of what education does for them? How can we help strengthen the understanding our students have of this, as well as their commitment to making the most of the educational opportunities they have?

MINI-SCENARIOS

Mini-scenario Number 1. A first grade teacher had planned to have his first grade students put a small trellis together from a kit. This trellis would be added to a small planter, seeds would be planted, and the students would observe and follow the sprouting of the seed and the growth of the plants. The kits were distributed. Students began to complete the project. The teacher expected the students to read the instructions on the kit and follow them with the assembly of their trellis. I noticed one little boy who was actually doing it backward. The longer pieces were supposed to be used on the bottom so that the circumference of the trellis would get smaller toward the top. The teacher noticed that the child was doing it incorrectly but he did nothing, letting the student continue his task. At one point, the first grade student looked around at his classmates and commented, "I did it wrong." At that point, the teacher went to the student to help guide his problem solving. The student again said, "I did it wrong." The teacher asked, "What do you think you should do about it?" The student picked up the instructions and began to read them again. The teacher watched him take his trellis apart and begin again. He then left to help other students. Once students were finished with the project and had planted the seeds, they left, by themselves, to go out to the playground where the planters would be able to be watered and get sunlight. The teacher did not go with them.

Mini-scenario Number 2. Knowing that students from America would be visiting their school, a second grade teacher made plans to use the American students in her lessons. One lesson was a lesson about common insects. She collected pictures of the insects. When the lesson began, she made three columns on the blackboard. The label of the first column was, "Japanese Word." The label for the second column was, "Picture of Insect," and the third was, "English Word." She then would show a picture of the insect. They would discuss it and then she would put the picture in the second column on the board, write the Japanese word for it, and ask our students how to say the English word for that insect. Students would then talk to the American teachers about the insect and what they knew.

Mini-scenario Number 3. Third grade students had just completed an assignment to determine which figures on their paper were congruent. All students had been assigned to work the same problem. The teacher asked three of them to come to the board and put their answers on the board. They were to say which figures were congruent and how they determined their answers. Each student explained his work and thinking about the problem in turn. At the end of the explanation, each student turned to his/her classmates and asked them what they thought about his/her solution to the problem. A discussion ensued. One student asked one of the students at the board why he hadn't considered a more common way to solve the problem. That began a very rich discussion about what it means to be congruent and how we can know when geometric shapes are congruent. By then, the period was over and students were ready to prepare for lunch. A group of students, however, stayed to talk with the teacher about the question that had been raised during the math discussions. This discussion continued for about 15 minutes.

Mini-scenario Number 4. A fifth grade class was reading a story entitled, "The Nest of Evil." Children had noticed a nest in a tree. Their parents had warned them not to go look at the nest because it was the nest of evil and bad things would happen if anyone tried to reach into the nest. The class had read to the point in the story where the children had, indeed, climbed the tree and were just ready to reach into the nest. The teacher asked the questions, "How do you think the children are feeling right now? Why?" The students discussed that one question for 40 minutes. A student would give his/her response and then the class would discuss it. The teacher said very little during this discussion. Class leaders called on those who wanted to share. A short summary of each point made was recorded on the board. At the end of the period, the teacher emphasized the major points presented in the discussion and prepared the students for the next reading assignment in the story.

Mini-scenario Number 5. We visited a brand new, full-size elementary school in a small community in the mountains above Osaka. We were shocked to find that there were only 27 students in the whole school. The citizens of the community were concerned that families were leaving their village and moving down into Osaka because there were more jobs and opportunities available. They wondered what they could do to encourage people to stay in the community. They decided to build a brand new school. It was just like all the other schools in Japan. It had rooms to support at least three classes in every grade, one through six. It had a gymnasium and a swimming pool. It had an art room and a music room. It even had a cafeteria, which is not usually the case in elementary schools in Japan. They continued to offer the full curriculum even though there were only 27 students in the entire school.

Mini-scenario Number 6. Students at all levels take a home economics course. It is very common to see fifth grade students learning how to sew on buttons. Elementary students also study color coordination in clothing. In the middle school, boys and girls take home economic courses. We were the beneficiaries of the lunch that the middle school class had cooked. We watched them prepare the meal. Students had access to everything they needed to cook the meal including butcher knives, paring knives, real gas stoves and ovens, etc.

Mini-scenario Number 7. As students first come to the preschool, they have active learning time. They are free to engage in any activities available. Doors to classrooms open to the outside where there are animals and a playground. At any given moment, we watched 3, 4, and 5 year olds riding unicycles on the playground, running and playing, playing in the sand pile, getting water to make mud in the sand pile, pulling a wagon up to the top of a hill in the middle of the playground, getting in and riding down (the hill was probably 15 feet high), using a huge knife to cut up lettuce to feed to the rabbits and goat. We also saw teachers working with individual children and small groups helping them learn specific things. One teacher was talking with children as they kneaded clay, molding it into shapes. Another teacher was helping students learn a song near the piano. Other students were painting on a huge mural that was being constructed about sea life. A huge piece of paper covered the blackboard and students could paint on the mural as they desired. Other children were taking cardboard they had brought to school, cutting it in long strips and using it to build a railroad track running through several classrooms. One little boy (5 years old) took me by the hand and asked if I wanted to look at the shells with him. He took me to a place in the room where there was a bucket of shells. He picked one up and showed me. I asked him the name of the shell. He thought for a minute. When he couldn't come up with the name, he ran just outside the classroom where the students had a rack on which they hung their caps and book bags. Each child had a hook. Also on the hook for each child were some field books. He grabbed his copy of the shell book, came back to me and scanned through the book until he found a picture of the shell he had. We then talked about the name of the shell and what animal had made it. We did that with several shells. He then picked up a rock that was in the same bucket. He said, "I don't think this is a shell. What do you think?" I said it didn't look like a shell. He ran back to the cap rack and grabbed his copy of the field book about rocks. He scanned through the pictures until he found a picture of the rock he had. It actually was a piece of granite. We talked about granite. He said, "I was right. It isn't a shell." We watched another boy take a small net and fish a goldfish out of the pond. He was proud of his catch and was taking it to everyone he could to show them that he had a goldfish. Finally, one of the teachers came up to him and said that if he didn't get it back into the water soon, it would die. They talked briefly about how fish need water to live. The teacher didn't make him put it back. The boy thought about it for a while and then went to put it back. By that time, however, the fish had died. The young boy felt badly. There was a tub that had crayfish in it. The students were able to pick up the crayfish and look at them. One little girl had a crayfish in one hand and a 2-inch minnow in the other. She was trying to force the minnow into the mouth of the crayfish. A teacher went to the crayfish area and talked about what crayfish eat. She asked if the girl thought the crayfish could eat a minnow that big.

Mini-scenario Number 8. Students in Japan, especially in the elementary and middle schools, clean the school each day right after lunch. They each have an assignment and will grab a broom, mop, dust rag, or other cleaning materials, go to their assigned spot in the building and spend 20-30 minutes cleaning the school.

Mini-scenario Number 9. Every year at one elementary school, fourth grade students plant rice in a field close to the school. A local farmer donates the plot each year. Teachers have added this to the curriculum to help students understand this part of their culture. At the same school, the fifth grade students harvest the rice when it is ready. They each take a small bag of rice home to cook and eat with their family. They send the rest of the rice to a country that is in need of food.

Mini-scenario Number 10. Swimming lessons are a part of the curriculum in Japanese schools. In fact, every school, elementary, middle, and high school, has a pool. Students take swim lessons each week during the spring. Sixth grade students at one elementary school could take a challenge to swim a mile in the ocean.

Mini-scenario Number 11. On one visit to an elementary school, we were impressed with an operetta that students were practicing. It was based on the book, *Swimmy*, by Leo Lionni. It was a remarkable operetta. Our teachers were very impressed and asked the Japanese teachers where they got the score for the operetta. They replied, "We wrote it, of course." Elementary teachers in Japan must be able to play the piano in order to get a job as a teacher. At a middle school, we were able to observe a chorus class. We were all very much impressed with how beautifully the students sang. We were amazed at the harmony. Our students were shocked to find out that this wasn't the middle school choir but simply one of their music classes that every student takes.

Mini-scenario Number 12. At least weekly, if not daily, all participants in the school meet in the gymnasium or on the playground for a morning assembly. The principal talks to the students, they sing a few songs, make announcements, celebrate any successes they have had, and get ready for the day.

Mini-scenario Number 13. Schools in Japan operate on a schedule of 50-minute periods. They meet for 50 minutes and have a 10-minute break. Then, they meet for 50 minutes and have a 20-minute break. Another 50-minute period and a 10-minute break. During the breaks, students are not supervised. They can stay in the classroom, wander the halls, go outside and play, etc. Teachers go to the teacher's room and prepare or collaborate with other teachers.

Mini-scenario Number 14. One elementary school was preparing to celebrate their 100th year as a school. They invited the community around the school to participate. Each business around the school did something at their establishment to help celebrate and help children gain a better sense of the history of the community. Some families whose homes were close to the school did a museum in their home to highlight part of their history. During the week, teachers took students to these businesses and homes. They had a huge assembly to celebrate. Each grade performed a musical number. At the end, a group of parents sang. The teachers wrote a special song for the occasion.

<u>Mini-scenario Number 15</u>. One day we planned to eat lunch at a preschool. The principal of the school had prepared the gymnasium for our lunch. She had put desks in groups of four throughout the gymnasium. When we went to lunch, she seated us so that one university student from North Carolina was in a group of three preschool children. It was a fascinating experience. She wanted her students to be able to interact with a foreigner—someone who didn't speak Japanese. One group of preschool children asked their guest, "Do you like Japanese food?" Of course, they asked the question in Japanese. The American students did not understand any Japanese and did not respond. The students repeated the question. Still no response from the American. The students then asked the question again. This time however, they asked it very slowly, "Do….you…like…Japanese…food?" No answer. Then the children asked the question in a very loud voice. It was a very interesting encounter.

<u>Mini-scenario Number 16</u>. One day, we were visiting one of the famous temples in Nara. Around the temple there are deer that roam. They like to come up to the visitors to try to get some food. We noticed that part of a preschool class had become separated from their teacher. The teacher had left the sidewalk and gone up a small hill to sit down and prepare for the picnic they had planned. Some of the class had been able to go with her. The rest of the class got cut off from the class because some of the deer had come to beg for food. The teacher did not seem concerned at all. It was almost as if she knew the students could handle it. The university students from America could not. They felt like they needed to intervene so that these children could get past the deer and rejoin their teacher. After jumping in, they realized that they might have taken away a good opportunity for problem solving.

<u>Mini-scenario Number 17</u>. One Japanese teacher said, "Children don't come to school to learn. They come to be with their friends. Therefore, if I can ensure that each child has a friend, feels part of a group, and knows they are making a positive contribution in the group, then learning will happen."

<u>Mini-scenario Number 18</u>. While meeting with a principal of one of the Pre-K schools we were visiting, one of our students asked, "What do you do to ensure that your students gain all the skills they will need to be ready for 1st grade?" The principal replied, "Oh, we don't do that here. We see our job as supporting the natural curiosity that our children have for nature and the world around them. We work to help them discover who they are."

Let's remember some of the comments from UNCW students who have traveled to Japan. These were listed in Chapter 1 and might shed more light on our understanding of our craft and what we should be about as we try to accomplish the incredible work of the elementary school.

"I learned that technology doesn't drive education, passion does."

"They seem to structure less but control more. They are able to let go and let the children be responsible."

"It is amazing how much more they do with music and art in their schools."

"I am impressed with the teachers' belief in the innate goodness of children."

"There is a pervading atmosphere of trust and respect. The Japanese people truly trust their children."

"I discovered what I must teach my own students. Hopefully I can help them understand our American need for forgiveness."

"I left the schools every day wondering if we expect too much from our children. We expect them to do things beyond their realm, but do not give them the independence and freedom to do it. We don't want to give them responsibility because they are children, but then expect them to act like they are little adults. We expect them to work to national standards, but do not give them time to master the skills to do so."

Likewise, comments Japanese students and teachers have made as they visited our schools can facilitate our discussion. Some of these were also listed in Chapter 1.

"Why are American teachers so quick to discipline? Why do American teachers have so many "don'ts" in their rooms?"

"Why is PE class talk, talk, talk, talk, talk, talk, do?"

When our students discovered that Japanese schools rarely, if ever, retain students in the same grade, they asked a principal what would be done if a school simply wasn't producing the student achievement that was expected. The principal answered, very matter-of-factly, "We'd probably hire more teachers to help."

"We look to America as the center for democracy. However, when we look at your schools, we don't see democracy at work. Where do students have the chance to practice and learn the principles of democracy?"

When a high school principal was asked how they screen the computers so students can't go to forbidden sites, he said, "We don't put a screen on the computer, we attempt to put the screen on the heart of the child, so they can use the computer responsibly."

Opportunity *for* dialogue:

What principles about our craft and how we should operate can you take from the vignettes above? Do you agree with those principles? How might they look in our schools? Do you think we could actually do what the Japanese teachers do?

PRINCIPLES:

Some principles we can learn from other cultures might include the following:
1. Children learn best by doing. If we can get children engaged in meaningful engagements for real purposes, their learning will be enhanced.
2. Children can benefit from having time to relax and take a breather—time to regroup—time to socialize. Recess might be an essential part of an effective learning classroom.

3. There is value in working hard to build a sense of community. Students can learn so much from being part of the healthy learning environment. They also can accelerate their own learning about the world by working together.

4. Teachers should be about the business of developing a positive, supportive rapport with students.

5. So much growth can happen if students and families have respect for education and understand what it can do for them. Educators in schools would be wise to help develop this understanding.

6. Learning is, in and of itself, exciting and generative.

7. We can trust students. We must trust them. This involves seeing them as capable, competent learners. Teachers are more effective when they can trust students, and when they can trust themselves and their own abilities. Trusting means letting go and not controlling so much.

8. Focusing on the why—focusing on the process can be supportive of learning.

9. There must be more to school than simple academics. We should also be helping prepare our students for other aspects of life. We can help them gain a strong work ethic, moral character, tolerance of others, the ability to forgive, understanding of what it means to be a responsible, contributing citizen, and the capacity to get along with everyone.

10. We probably can help our students take on more responsibility than we do.

11. It can be very helpful to provide more opportunities for our students to explore the world through other sign systems such as art, music, drama, etc.

12. We would do well to better understand our roles as teachers—are we nurturers or tamers?

13. We can have higher expectations for our students than we do. Those expectations should be more than scores on tests or other academic achievement. Perhaps our expectations could also include preparation for life.

14. Perhaps we can be more effective in our teaching if we try to teach less but organize our classrooms to support our children in learning more.

Opportunity *for* dialogue:

As you review the principles listed above, what implications do you see for our elementary schools? What implications do you see for your role as a teacher? What implications do you see for the way we assess our students?

ELEMENTARY PROGRAMS AND PRACTICES
EDN 300
OPPORTUNITY FOR DIALOGUE

Name:

Chapter:

CHAPTER four

Classroom Management:
A Teacher's Story

> The mediocre teacher tells.
> The good teacher explains. The
> superior teacher demonstrates.
> The great teacher inspires.
>
> —William Arthur Ward

Chapter 2 included a detailed discussion of constructivist and behaviorist instruction. A constructivist philosophy suggests that teachers empower students as learners, help them find their own voices, and help them take ownership in order to help make the learning more meaningful for students. The belief here is that learning takes place internally. A behaviorist philosophy suggests that instruction is carefully broken down into small, successive steps to best assist students to master a hierarchy of skills. Behaviorism focuses on measurable changes. The belief here is that all behavior results from an external stimulus. These concepts are important to remember in a discussion about classroom management.

What follows is a shortened version of my story as a new elementary school teacher, and an analysis of lessons learned. The hope is that my story will provide the basis for classroom dialogue and questioning. My first year as an elementary teacher was a learning experience in terms of classroom management. As a student teacher, I had been responsible for 19 second-graders, with help from a teacher assistant and my cooperating teacher. As a first-year teacher, I was assigned a classroom of 29 third-graders, with a teacher assistant in the classroom one day a week. I was 22 years old, and I was sure the kids would respect me because I was "young and cool." I misinterpreted my constructivist-leaning philosophical stance to mean that the students would develop a respect for me if I went out of my way to make sure they liked me. I learned later that a respected teacher can earn his or her "coolness," but a "cool" teacher is not automatically respected. As a result, my classroom management was poor. The students walked all over me for weeks. At a low point, I exclaimed to my class upon returning from lunch, "I am not going to begin teaching until I have complete silence!" I waited for silence until the final bell rang.

On Fridays, the teacher assistant was present in my classroom. The students loved her. She was from the community, and had been at the school for years. My students displayed model behavior on Fridays, they did not want to disappoint her, and her discipline was firm. She was a stark reminder of what I lacked during those first weeks. There is an unfortunate tendency for teachers to place the blame for an out-of-control classroom on their students, when a cursory look at the same students' behavior with other adults paints a different picture. I was not in denial of my deficiencies, and no teacher should be. Who is perfect at any job on Day 1? Although a blow to my ego, this recognition was a necessary step in my early development as a teacher.

Needless to say, something had to change. I rethought and revamped my classroom management system in the coming months and even more in the following year. By my third year teaching, I was confident in my system, and was glad when the "tough" students were assigned to me. By then, I evoked the same response from my students that only my teacher assistant had evoked early in year one. Below I will take you through my journey, and describe the evolution and rationale of what became a successful behavior management system. This is certainly not to say that my techniques are the only successful ones, instead it is meant only to share one successful experience:

I started a new system the third month of school, after I came to the realization that my classroom management up to that point had been subpar. This was a task in and of itself – the kids had been used to 3 months of inconsistency, with no real policy in place. My cooperating teacher had used "stick-flipping" and "card-pulling" techniques for behavior management. I saw a lot of this throughout my undergraduate

_____ 's Responsibility Sheet for the week of _____

Behavior   ### Homework

Monday [ ]   [ ]

Tuesday [ ]   [ ]

KEY:

GREEN
Excellent/
Satisfactory

YELLOW
Borderline/
Incomplete or
Incorrect

RED
Unsatisfactory/
F or Zero

Wednesday [ ]   [ ]

Thursday [ ]   [ ]

Friday [ ]   [ ]

Bonus Boxes: [ ] [ ] [ ] [ ] [ ]

Student Signature _____ Date_____

Parent Signature _____ Date_____

Comments:

field experiences, and although I did not imagine myself a behaviorist, I began there. I created a pocket chart complete with every student's name and a supply of colored Popsicle sticks. Each time a student broke a rule, they were asked to flip their stick to a new color. They began the day on green, which represented "excellent." After a warning, the first flip resulted in a yellow stick ("borderline"), and finally after another flip they were on red ("unsatisfactory"). I combined this with my already-in-place homework reporting sheet. At the end of each week, the students colored their days and brought the sheets home to their parents to be signed (see record sheet 1).

I ran into several unanticipated problems with this system. This was something new for the students; I had no real behavior plan in place before, and they were resistant to change. Asking a student to flip their stick was often met with an angry response. When a student was angry, asking them to flip their stick was often a disruption. Not only was it a likely embarrassment for the student to have their poor behavior on display for anyone who may enter the room, but it was a chance for attention seekers to get attention by either refusing to flip, or skipping, dancing, pouting, or mumbling their way to their stick to flip it. Secondly, once a student was on "red," there was no external incentive to behave for the remainder of the day. I tried to remedy this through the inclusion of the "bonus boxes," but boy, did that make extra work for me! Thirdly, I placed a difficult onus on myself to be consistent, and have eyes everywhere. For example, if one student flipped their stick for cutting in line, I had to be sure to catch every other line-cutter, or else the student who flipped would feel as though he were singled out unfairly. Lastly, the record-keeping process was a pain. Every day! Sometimes I just wanted to go home after work.

These problems brought about a second incarnation of my record sheet during year two (see sheet 2). This time I was able to begin on the first day of school. Although I continued recording each day's homework on the record sheet (this had been successful in the previous year), I changed my behavior management technique altogether. Based on the previous year's experience, I eliminated the stick-flipping. Instead, at the end of each week, I wrote each parent a note concerning their child's behavior for the week. This involved a tremendous amount of record keeping and writing. Additionally, students with negative comments were less likely to bring their sheets home, which would usually result in phone calls, rendering my hours of writing comments pointless.

_____ 's Responsibility Sheet for the week of _____

Homework

Monday   [ ]

Tuesday   [ ]   **KEY:**

                       GREEN
                       Excellent/
                       Satisfactory

Wednesday   [ ]
                       YELLOW
                       Borderline/
                       Incomplete or
                       Incorrect
Thursday   [ ]

                       RED
                       Unsatisfactory/
                       F or Zero
Friday   [ ]

Teacher comments:

Student Signature _____ Date_____
Parent Signature _____ Date_____
Parent comments:

Although my classroom management (and parent communication) had improved from the previous year, I was still not consistently getting the behavior that I expected from my class. I knew they were capable of it, because I had observed it with other teachers and assistants. As humbling as that was, I knew the onus was on me. Up to this point, my classroom rules were the typical rules you may find in any elementary classroom: Raise your hand to speak, keep your hands to yourself, treat others the way you would like to be treated, etc. These rules had become so routine for the students, I wondered whether they needed a change. For example, I asked myself whether I always expected students to raise their hands to speak, or was it appropriate to speak without raising their hands at some points? What was my rule for turning in homework, going to the restroom, etc.? My expectations were unclear at best, and non-existent at worst. During my third summer as a teacher, I read *Ron Clark's Essential 55*. Ron Clark is an elementary teacher from North Carolina who won Disney's National Teacher of the Year award. He shared 55 rules that he used with his students. His expectations were clear and specific. This was what I was looking for. Some of his rules were as follows:

- **Rule 8:** Do not smack your lips, tsk, roll your eyes, or show disrespect with gestures.
- **Rule 13:** When we read together in class, you must follow along. If I call on you to read, you must know exactly where we are and begin to read immediately.
- **Rule 14:** Answer all questions with a complete sentence. For example, if the question asks, "What is the capital of Russia?" you should respond by writing, "The capital of Russia is Moscow." Also, in conversation with others, it is important to use complete sentences out of respect for the person's question. For example, if a person asks, "How are you?" instead of just responding by saying, "Fine," you should say, "I'm doing fine, thank you. How about yourself?"
- **Rule 16:** Homework will be turned in each day for each subject by every student with no exceptions.
- **Rule 21:** We will follow certain classroom protocols. We will be organized, efficient, and on task. In order to do so, we will follow these rules: 1. Do not get out of your seat without permission. Exception: If you are sick, leave immediately. 2. Do not speak unless: You raise your hand, and I call on you. I ask you a question and you are responding. It is a recess or lunch. I instruct you otherwise (for example, during group work).
- **Rule 45:** Never cut line. If someone cuts in front of you, do not say or do anything about it. Let it happen, but let me know about it. I will handle the situation. If you fuss with someone who has cut in line, you could get in trouble as well. It's not worth it; just let me know what happened. Please handle all disputes with other classmates in the same manner, by coming to me with any problems before you take matters into your own hands.

Source: The Essential 55 by Ron Clark. Copyright © 2003 by Ron Clark.

Boy, were Mr. Clark's expectations hard to misinterpret. I began the following year with a similar set of rules. I had my new students complete attention when going over them the first day of school, as it took nearly the whole day. I used my best "I mean business" voice, but I didn't forget to smile. Mr. Clark's rule number 47 was,

"Do not bring Doritos in the school building." He complimented it with a story about why he hated Doritos and was very serious about it. The goal was to add some humor and personality to the rules. Following suit, one of my rules was, "Absolutely no Hot Cheetos allowed." Hot Cheetos were a favorite snack of my students, and not of mine. When I got some giggles and questions about my level of seriousness regarding that specific rule, I told the students that it was one of the most important rules (with a smile)—about how I had to sit for years watching students eat a snack I hate, and that I was very serious about it. I let them know that I would crush any Hot Cheetos that I saw to dust. The students smiled, realizing that there was more to me than a list of rules, and that they might actually have some fun this year. (Side note: At least one student brought Hot Cheetos to school in almost every day for lunch, and every day I crushed them, resulting in smiles. To this day, former students contact me about my dislike for Hot Cheetos. Funny thing is, they aren't even that bad.)

Also, I had finally mastered my behavior plan. No more flipping sticks, no more long notes to each parent each week that rarely found their way home. Instead, I became known for my clipboards: One was a homework clipboard and one was a behavior clipboard (see tally charts). I had always used some variation of the homework clipboard, with different symbols representing completed, incomplete, late, or missing homework. Now that my expectations were clear, I had 2 symbols; students received a check each day that homework was completed, and a 0 each day that it was incomplete or missing. These translated to green or red boxes on my new, streamlined record sheet (see sheet 3). In case you are wondering, the numbers on the chart represented their place in line—no more debate over cutting in line, they were in the same place every time.

Dr. Wasserberg's 4th Grade Class (Rm. 1030):					
		Homework Tally			
	Name:	week 1	week 2	week 3	comments
		M T W R F	M T W R F	M T W R F	
6	Jennifer Garcia				
19	Alejandra Gomez				
1	Ethel Lam				
2	Mason Carter				
11	Chase Justice				
17	Dylan James				

The behavior clipboard was a new system of mine that was successful for all my remaining years in the classroom. Student behavior was no longer displayed for the class. I developed a chart on which students would receive tally marks every time they broke a rule, after one warning. One tally mark brought their behavior grade for the week from an A to a B, two tally marks brought their behavior grade for the week from a B to a C, and so on. Students were able to earn back a half grade (a B could be bumped up to an A- by the end of the week). Students did not see their tally count until grades were recorded on Fridays. Just picking up the board usually put an end to any incorrect behaviors. Interestingly, the sheer mystery of it sometimes brought about confessions:

Denise: Dr. Wasserberg, do I have any tally marks this week?

Dr. W: What do you think, Denise, should you have any this week?

Denise: Well, I guess you saw me kick Joshua earlier, sorry.

Dr. W: Yes, Denise. I see everything, you have one behavior mark, but I am sure you will improve this week. (I proceed to add the behavior mark).

Denise: Okay, Dr. W.

Dr. Wasserberg's 4th Grade Class (Rm. 1030):					
		Behavior Tally			
	Name:	*week 1*	*week 2*	*week 3*	*comments*
6	Jennifer Garcia				
19	Alejandra Gomez				
1	Ethel Lam				
2	Mason Carter				
11	Chase Justice				
17	Dylan James				

After years of trial and error, what would be the final version of my record sheet had also been established. Checks and zeros translated to greens or reds for homework, and behavior marks translated to a weekly behavior grade written in the behavior box. Perfect record sheets earned weekly rewards, and students brought home record sheets to be signed every Friday. This became my (very behaviorist) individual reward system. I also had a reward points system for table groups and whole class. A respectful environment with clear expectations was ultimately established in my classroom.

_____'s Weekly Report (week of _____) _____

Homework

	Monday
	Tuesday
	Wednesday
	Thursday
	Friday

HOMEWORK KEY:

GREEN
All homework completed

RED
Homework Incomplete
or Missing

BEHAVIOR BOX:

Student Signature _____ Date_____

Parent Signature _____ Date_____

Comments:

Looking back, I call this my "behaviorist front." This clear system of rules, rewards and punishments created an orderly, safe classroom environment. But the goal of classroom management should be more than that. My students were behaving well because they knew the rules, wanted the rewards, and wanted to avoid punishment. I knew that wouldn't last—rewards get old, punishments get repetitive. I wanted to teach my students to *care*—teach them to behave respectfully; not for a reward, but because it was the right thing to do. This is the incredible work of an elementary school teacher.

Now here is the missing piece of this story: After my rules and behavior plan had clearly been established, by the third month, I rarely needed my clipboards. By the end of the year, I couldn't tell you where they were...

Opportunity *for*
dialogue:

Discuss some classroom management techniques you have observed and/or experienced. What worked, what didn't? Finally, before reading on, why do you think my clipboards became irrelevant by the middle of a successful year?

By the third month, I had developed positive relationships with my students, and my classroom management became much more constructivist in nature. That is, my class became self-disciplined, as opposed to being extrinsically controlled.

Mini-Scenario:

Mr. Wasserberg assigned Jennifer, one of his most trustworthy students as homework recorder this week. It was her responsibility to collect homework, and place checks by the names of those who had turned it in.

As the class left the room for lunch, Jennifer was finishing up this task. Upon a quick glance, Mr. Wasserberg noticed that Jennifer had placed a check next to her friend Erica's name. Mr. Wasserberg knew Erica had not completed her homework. He asked Jennifer, "Did Erica do her homework today?" giving her an inquisitive look. Jennifer's face dropped as her eyes welled up with tears. She loved her teacher, and she knew she had violated his trust. She could barely eke out an "I'm sorry." Mr. Wasserberg saw in her face that she would never do it again.

Opportunity *for*
dialogue:

In the above scenario, would it be necessary to give Jennifer a "behavior mark" for her actions? Why or why not?

Behavioral boundaries had clearly been established through rewards and punishment. Now, I put in work for months developing positive relationships with my students. This means more than smiling as your students come in the door (although that is important as well), but really getting to *know* your students. My first recommendation would be to eat lunch with your class at least a few times a week. The conversations at the lunchroom table are a real chance to learn about your kids—who plays on the same football team, who goes to church together, and who hates chocolate ice cream. All of these tidbits of information gave me a chance to bond and relate to my students.

"I like football, too, I used to play quarterback."
"Oh, that church is near my house."
"What you hate chocolate ice cream!? That's my favorite."

This is particularly important when teaching children with social experiences that are different from your own. Let's think closely about why that may be. It is much easier to relate to someone with similar experiences. Think about your circle of friends. It is likely you have similar tastes in music, sports, clothes, conversation topics, restaurants, etc. That is at least part of what makes your relationship work. Think about how difficult it would be to maintain a friendship with someone with whom you had none of these things in common. You wouldn't be able to discuss your favorite songs, eat happily at the same restaurants, shop at the same stores, or even talk about anything of substance. However, this is exactly what you will have to do with your students, regardless of whether they grew up like you did, look like you did or act like you did. Taking the time to build relationships and bond with your students gives them a window into your world as well. Once I got to know my students, rewards such as candy and stickers were replaced with assigning students jobs that I knew they loved, and tally marks next to names were replaced with discussions with students that ended with a mutual understanding. This is not to say that all of my behavior problems disappeared, by any means. However, my behavior chart disappeared because when a student misbehaved, they knew that they had disappointed me; they no longer needed a behavior mark to tell them that. Disappointing me only mattered to them because I had developed positive relationships with them. They cared about their behavior, and they cared about my opinion about their behavior. The flow chart above represents a breakdown of the described process toward successful classroom management. Many teachers considered successful disciplinarians never progress past block two.

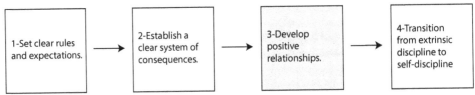

| 1-Set clear rules and expectations. | → | 2-Establish a clear system of consequences. | → | 3-Develop positive relationships. | → | 4-Transition from extrinsic discipline to self-discipline |

Opportunity *for* dialogue: What is the difference between a classroom that has reached step 2 of this process, and one that has reached step 4?

ELEMENTARY PROGRAMS AND PRACTICES
EDN 300
OPPORTUNITY FOR DIALOGUE

Name:

Chapter:

CHAPTER five
Elements of Diversity

"If students are products of experience, it would be wise to know their experience and begin from there."

– John Dewey

As an elementary teacher, you will be responsible for a diverse group of learners. **Diversity** encompasses socioeconomics, race, gender, nationality, language, (dis) abilities, sexual orientation, and more. A true understanding of diversity involves understanding how your students perceive themselves, how you perceive your students, and how your students perceive you. Sound confusing? Ok, let's break down what these mean in terms of diversity.

How your students perceive themselves: What are your students' beliefs regarding diversity. Do they believe themselves to be intrinsically "better" or "worse" than other students in your classroom? Is their self-esteem tied to their socioeconomic status, race, gender, etc.? Do they discriminate against peers based on any of these characteristics?

How you perceive your students: Do you harbor any stereotypes? Are your actions toward your students related to stereotypical thoughts about the groups they belong to? Have you gotten to know your students well enough to judge them as individuals?

How your students perceive you: Whether or not you harbor any stereotypes, do your students have any reason to believe you may? Do your students feel comfortable enough in your classroom to be themselves? Do you treat all of your students fairly?

It is a teacher's responsibility to work for all of those perceptions to be positive ones, as those perceptions will have a direct influence on classroom interactions. This is the incredible work of an elementary school teacher.

For an elementary classroom to be a welcoming environment, teachers need to be able to positively interact with a diverse group of children. As discussed in the previous chapter, this is particularly important when teaching children with social experiences and characteristics that are different from your own. In North Carolina, Professional Teaching Standard 2 requires that *Teachers establish a respectful environment for a diverse population of students.* "Elements of Diversity" could easily be the title for an entire textbook, or an entire course, for that matter. What follows is an overview of some major topics related to elementary schools.

SOCIOECONOMICS:

Tasks:

Task 1: In class, divide your money <u>equally</u> amongst your group.

Task 2: Divide the money <u>fairly</u> amongst your group.

Opportunity *for* dialogue:

Did you have different outcomes? What is the difference between these 2 statements?

What will be your goal in your classroom? Will you strive to treat each student the same (equally) or will you strive to treat each student fairly by responding to their individual diverse set of needs (**equitably**)?

In the context of the public school system, equality amongst schools refers to dividing resources equally, while equity amongst schools refers to dividing resources fairly. In the United States, property taxation and local school funding are closely linked. A large percentage of all property tax revenue is utilized for K-12 public education. This may account for vast disparities in public school funding, depending on the tax base of the community. Elementary schools PTAs are also known for fund-raising. Think back, do you remember selling candy or magazines door-to-door, bake sales, or carnival days? Well one can imagine the disparity in revenues that such events can generate depending on the community the school serves. As an example, there a number of elementary schools in New Hanover County that have purchased things like SmartBoards for each classroom without dipping into their budgets, using only PTA generated funds, while others do not have that luxury.

In addition to between-school socioeconomic diversity, there will undoubtedly be socioeconomic diversity within your own classroom. Below are some elementary school scenarios:

- Travon comes to school as the bell rings, in unwashed clothes. He immediately snaps at a classmate and puts his head down on his desk.
- Carol shuts down when she gets handed a red and green crayon for her journaling assignment. "I wanted purple!" she pouts.
- Danilo steals an extra bag of chips from the lunch line. He slips them into his book bag, and is sent to the principal by the lunch monitor.

Insightful Teacher Quote:

> *If students are products of experience, it would be wise to know their experience and begin from there.*
> John Dewey

Now, none of these behaviors are acceptable. However, how a teacher chooses to deal with these scenarios may be different depending on the student. The teacher should be fair and equitable, but not necessarily equal. It may sound nice to say "I treat all of my students the same," but your students will not be the same, different students require different things. The quote from renowned educator John Dewey (above) is applicable here. Let's take a look at these students' experiences:

- Travon is the oldest son in a single-parent household. His mother leaves to work before dawn. Travon has to get his younger brothers ready for school. Sometimes, he doesn't have a chance to get ready himself, and he does not want his brothers to be late.
- Carol comes from a wealthy family. Her parents are divorced and compete for her attention. She is an only child, and is used to getting anything she wants.
- Danilo is homeless. He sometimes goes to bed without dinner.

Opportunity *for* **dialogue:** How would knowing the experiences of these children change the way a teacher may deal with the scenarios above?

Socioeconomic status could have a strong impact on available home resources, school readiness, parental involvement, and student perspectives. Families from high socioeconomic status often have access to a wider range of resources that promote school success. These may include books, educational toys, and academic conversations. Additionally, these families often have had the opportunity to expose their children to a wider range of experiences, which may include travel and access to top-notch preschools. Families from lower socioeconomic statuses may lack the financial resources and time to provide this access to their children. (One should not confuse this lack of resources with a lack of care, however.) As a result, children from these families are sometimes less prepared for school when entering an elementary school setting. The onus is on the teacher to make accommodations to create a successful learning environment for all children.

RACE:

The academic performance (as measured by standardized tests) of African American, Latino, and Native American students, in comparison to their white and Asian counterparts, has long been a serious concern and source of debate. Much of the discourse focuses on a deficit model to explain the test score gap.[1] Such explanations, however, may downplay the effect of contextual forces over which a teacher has direct control. There are several examples where traditionally underperforming groups flourish, where a teacher has made the difference. This is the incredible work of an elementary school teacher.

Media Break:

On April 5, 1968 (the day following the assassination of Martin Luther King, Jr.), Jane Elliot initiated the first in a series of annual exercises on prejudice in her third grade classroom.

For a day, she made the blue-eyed children in her class "superior." She told them they were smarter, and she gave them several extra privileges, such as extra recess time, access to the better water fountain, and praise for their hard work. They were not allowed to play with the brown-eyed children. The "brown-eyes," on the other hand, were demeaned, criticized, and made to wear collars.

The following day, she reversed the exercise.

Interestingly, in both instances, those who were deemed "superior" became insulting and abusive toward their "inferior" classmates. Their

---

1 The term "test score gap" is used in place of "achievement gap" to indicate that it is solely in reference to gaps in standardized test scores, which are not the only measure of "achievement." The "achievement gap" characterization is problematic, in that it (a) infers that the burden for underperformance is solely students', and (b) it often uses white students' normative performance as a universal standard.

performance on academic tasks also improved considerably. The "inferior" children's academic performance faltered, even with tasks that had previously been simple for them.

A documentary chronicling the exercise is available for free viewing here: http://topdocumentaryfilms.com/a-class-divided/

This was, and still is, an amazing commentary on the influence of prejudice in the classroom.

Since Jane Elliot's exercise has gained national recognition, there has been much research supporting that when an elementary student feels they are being judged in terms of a stereotype, their academic performance suffers (e.g. McKown & Weinstein, 2003; Wasserberg, 2014). What can you do in your future classroom to avoid this perception from your diverse group of learners? The student-teacher relationship is an integral part of working toward a solution. Teachers who view their students in terms of their deficits, as opposed to their strengths, are unlikely to gain the trust of their students. Accomplished teacher and scholar Lisa Delpit puts it eloquently in the quote below.

Insightful Teacher Quote:

"I have discovered that children of color... seem especially sensitive to their relationship between themselves and their teacher. I have concluded that it appears that they not only learn from a teacher but also for a teacher. If they do not feel connected to a teacher on an emotional level, then they will not learn, they will not put out the effort." (2006, p. 227)

- "Practice for the state test this Friday," Ms. Baker says to her students. Chris, a high-performing African-American fifth grader, feels a wave of anxiety. In addition to the normal pressures a student feels when faced with a standardized test, Chris feels the additional pressures of not confirming negative stereotypes he has heard about his race. This additional pressure causes him to not finish the test.

Opportunity *for* dialogue:

How could Ms. Baker, who does not subscribe to stereotypes based on race, have helped to alleviate Chris' anxiety in this situation?

Racial stereotypes regarding academic performance can become salient and have adverse performance effects for children at early ages. These potential effects are disconcerting in a time when many school systems have drastically increased the significance of standardized testing in the elementary grades. Attention to the situational presentation of testing is therefore critical. Test performance is sensitive to situational and cognitive processes amenable to teacher intervention. I am sure all of us can remember a teacher who made test day extremely nerve-racking. Therefore, attention to the classroom environment is particularly important to teachers of students who are already subject to societal stereotyping. As a teacher one should consider the following question: What have I done to reassure students that societal stereotypes do not apply within my classroom walls?

Unfortunately, standardized test-based reforms have resulted in the labeling of many predominantly African-American and Latino schools as low-achieving. This discounts the children in those schools that are high-achievers while creating a context for perpetuating stereotypes by framing the test score gap as the sole basis for judgments about the academic abilities of African American and Latino students. Research findings (Wasserberg, 2014) demonstrate that the resulting environments in such schools heighten students' awareness of racial stereotypes, creating an environment susceptible to the detrimental performance effects similar to what you watched in the documentary. This of particular importance to teachers of African American and Latino children in that attention to the environmental details surrounding standardized testing situations can help create a more comfortable environment and potentially prevent negative performance consequences for their students.

Ladson-Billings (1995) and others have used the term **culturally relevant pedagogy** when referring to the pedagogy of successful teachers of racial minorities. Culturally relevant pedagogy can be described as creating a learning experience that allows students to excel without jeopardizing their cultural integrity. Simply put, teaching and learning take place within a framework that is consistent with the students' cultural background. Culturally relevant pedagogy is in part characterized by a teacher's willingness and ability to demonstrate a connectedness with all of his or her students, maintain positive relationships, develop a community of learners, and maintain fluid student-teacher relationships (Ladson-Billings, 1995). As stressed in the previous chapter, the component of culturally relevant pedagogy focused on maintenance of positive student-teacher relationships should be an integral part of any teacher's classroom. The caring teacher-student relationships have been shown to increase effort and improve academic performance (Delpit, 2006). For that reason alone, the development of such relationships should be a central facet of any teacher's classroom.

GENDER:

What are little boys made of?
Snips and snails, and puppy dogs tails
That's what little boys are made of!
What are little girls made of?
Sugar and spice and all things nice
That's what little girls are made of!

-Children's Rhyme

One day I was reading a story to my fourth grade students in my classroom, when I mentioned that a colleague of mine, a professor from the local university, would be stopping by this afternoon to visit. "Is it the same lady that came last month?" one of my students questioned. It was "the same lady," but before I could respond to the question, one of my girls cut in, "No, girls can't be professors!" I waited after that comment, and no students offered rebuttal. I was as bothered by their silence as I was by the comment. From that point a goal of mine became to work to eliminate stereotype-based perceptions in my classroom. I share this story in the hopes that this becomes one of your goals before it became one of mine.

Read the scenarios below. Think about why they might occur, and what a teacher should do when noticing something similar in his or her classroom.

- A kindergarten teacher is listening to his students' conversation during dress-up time that his students assign girls a smaller range of lesser-paying jobs than boys. "You can't be a doctor, Denise! You are a girl!" he hears Danielle say.
- A fourth grade teacher notices one of her girls, Aaliyah, hiding her A+ test score, and later insisting to her friends that she is "so bad at math."

Opportunity *for* dialogue:

How could these teachers work to combat gender stereotypes in their classrooms?

Stereotypes of gender inferiority pervade books, television, and other aspects of popular culture. Instead of expressing their individuality, children's characters ritually subscribe to gender stereotypes: *Teen-Talk Barbie's* electric voice box giggled "Math is hard! I love shopping! Will we ever have enough clothes?" *Dora the Explorer* (once a beacon of counter-stereotype for young girls) became *Dora's Explorer Girls*, largely, abandoning her love for outdoor exploration. To be sure, children's literature used in the elementary school is also often characterized by tough, strong boys; and damsels in distress exclaiming, "my hero." Fictional characters from children's literature used in elementary classrooms often embody gender stereotypes. Male characters are characterized as strong, aggressive, and in control, whereas female characters are often characterized as weak, passive, and dependent. It is not hard to understand how children may come to reflect these stereotypes in their attitudes and cognitions, especially when they exist in a context unlikely to offer counter-stereotype models.

Teachers may be unaware of subtle biases that manifest themselves in classrooms. Teachers should be cognizant of the gender bias embedded in many educational materials and texts, and need to combat this bias. One method could include the use of nontraditional gender role literature. Such literature should include the following: individuals portrayed with distinctive personalities not determined by their gender, achievements not evaluated on the basis of gender, occupations represented without gender bias, and individuals displaying emotion depending upon the situation, not on their gender. Additionally, combining traditional and nontraditional literature brings about classroom dialoguing on gender stereotypes. Many children's books can be used as catalysts for these dialogues, which can also work to build more positive relationships between students and teachers. This is the incredible work of an elementary school teacher. Following the comment made in my classroom referring to a female professor colleague, I initiated a unit with my students which combined traditional and nontraditional gender role literature. The resulting discussions went a long way to counter some stereotype-based perceptions held by my students.

> Throw out those glass slippers. Send the fairies to sleep. No prince is waiting for me. For if you look twice, past the sugar and spice, the eyes of a tiger you'll see.
>
> I Look Like a Girl (1999)

LANGUAGE DIVERSITY:

English language learners (ELLs) represent the fastest growing segment of the school-aged population in the United States. Projections suggest that students who speak a language other than English at home will comprise over 40% of K-12 students by 2030. Teachers of ELLs must accommodate their students. Suggested strategies include modeling, establishing cooperative learning groups, repetition, role-playing, activating prior knowledge, graphic organizers, etc. Importantly, each of these helpful strategies for the teaching of ELLs is also beneficial for all students. Luckily, great teachers already have these strategies in their everyday repertoire!

Successful techniques for teaching ELLs are the basis for entire books and courses of study. It is more than likely that your first classroom will include English language learners, and you are encouraged to pursue these sources of knowledge. What follows here is simply a cursory look at different placement options available for ELLs in elementary schools

- Submersion ("Sink or Swim"):
    ELLs are placed in the same classes as English speaking students and required to learn as much as they can (English–only).
- Pull-out:
    English learners are given a separate ELL class for a prescribed period of time, usually one hour per day. The students miss what is going on in the "regular class" during that time. The rest of the day is spent in the "regular class."
- ELL Class Period:
    ELLs have their English-language class in place of an elective, or as an alternative to language arts. They don't miss out on anything that happens in the "regular class."

- Sheltered English Immersion:

    General education teachers are considered the ELL teachers as well. At first glance, one may mistake a Sheltered English Immersion classroom for a Submersion classroom, however in Sheltered English Immersion classrooms teachers are required to make accommodations within each lesson to assist ELLs. Accommodations may include use of clear, direct language, hand-gestures, scaffolding techniques, learning activities that incorporate students' prior knowledge, and peer collaboration. These classrooms offer ELLs the content instruction of their English-speaking peers, while adapting lesson delivery to suit their English proficiency level.

- One-Way Bilingual Education:

    Bilingual program in which ELLs receive instruction in English and their native language, with a goal of learning English.

- Two-Way Bilingual Education:

    Bilingual program in which ELLs AND English-only speaking students receive instruction in English and the native language of the ELLs. The goal is for all students to become bilingual. (Student population is preferably 50% English-only speakers, and 50% ELLs).

It can't be repeated enough that as a teacher one of your primary responsibilities will be to make your students feel comfortable and safe. This may take some extra effort on your part if the student is unfamiliar with English. Some simple ways you can support your ELL student(s) are the following: have resources in the student's home language available in the classroom, allow the student to talk or write in their primary language when learning English, learn a few words in the students home language (better yet, let them teach you), and foster a sense of belonging for their families.

STUDENTS WITH DISABILITIES:

According to the National Center for Educational Statistics, nearly 14% of children in public schools are students with disabilities. Again, successful techniques for teaching Students with Disabilities are the basis for entire books and courses of study. It is more than likely that your first classroom will include Students with Disabilities, and you are encouraged to pursue these sources of knowledge. What follows here is simply a cursory look at different placement options available for Students with Disabilities in elementary schools

- Inclusion

    Student with disability is placed in a general education classroom. There would ideally be a special education teacher present whose job it would be to modify the curriculum to the abilities of the student.

- Pull-out (Resource)

    Students with disabilities are pulled-out during certain subjects to receive more intensive instruction in a self-contained classroom with other special needs education students.

- Self-Contained Classroom
  Students with disabilities are removed from the general education setting, and receive all instruction from a special education teacher in a small class setting. Class works at academic level of each individual student.
- Special School Placement
  Student with disability attends a school specifically designed to address their special learning or behavioral needs.

Types of disabilities recognized by the federal government include specific learning disabilities, speech or language impairments, mental retardation, visual impairments, hearing impairments, emotional disturbances, and autism, among others. Federal law requires schools to develop an Individualized Education Plan (IEP) for each student with a disability. Teachers, counselors, and parents work together to fill out and update IEPs each year for each student. The IEP is the basis of a student's educational program. By law, the IEP must include certain information about the student, the student's specific disability, and the educational program designed to meet his or her unique needs. This information includes performance on relevant assessments, short-term learning objectives, annual learning goals, special services to be provided, accommodations, placements, participation in state and district-wide tests, and measured progress. An IEP must be designed to meet the unique educational needs of that one child in the *Least Restrictive Environment* appropriate to the needs of that child. This is the incredible work of an elementary school teacher.

Delpit, L. (2006). Lessons from teachers. *Journal of Teacher Education, 57*(3), 220-231.

Ladson-Billings, G. (1995). Toward a theory of culturally relevant pedagogy. *American Educational Research Journal, 32*(3), 465-491.

McKown, C. & Weinstein, R. S. (2003). The development and consequences of stereotype consciousness in middle childhood. *Child Development, 74*(2), 498-515.

Wasserberg, M. J. (2014). Stereotype threat effects on African American children in an urban elementary school. *The Journal of Experimental Education, 82*(4), 502-517.

ELEMENTARY PROGRAMS AND PRACTICES
EDN 300
OPPORTUNITY FOR DIALOGUE

Name:

Chapter:

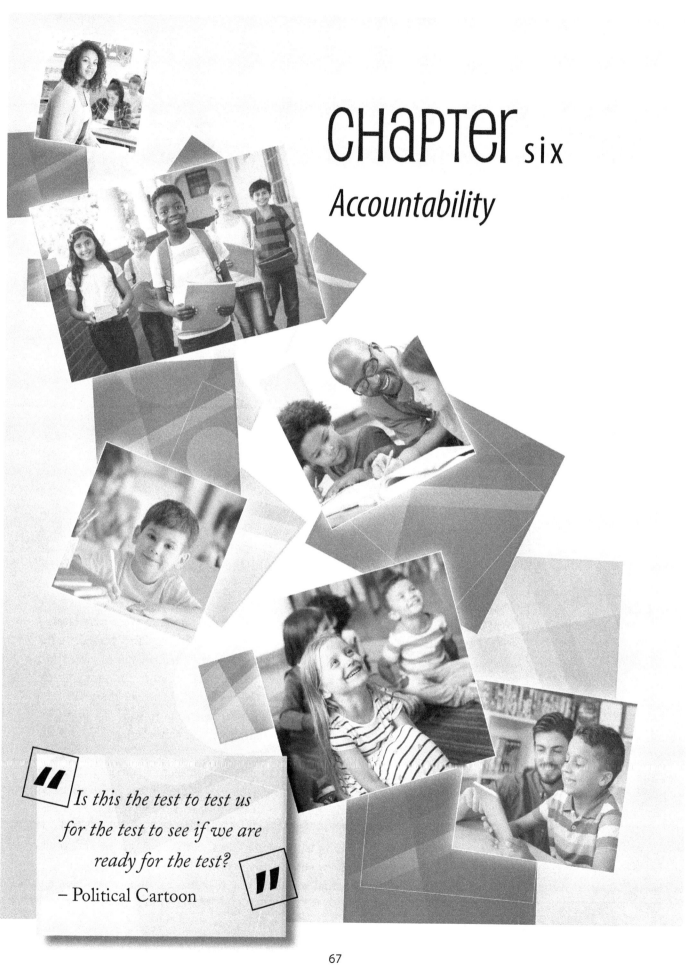

CHAPTER six
Accountability

"Is this the test to test us for the test to see if we are ready for the test?"

– Political Cartoon

Opportunity *for*
dialogue:

"Accountability" has become the most recent buzzword in education. It refers to the idea of holding teachers, administrators, schools, and districts responsible for student achievement. Most often, "student achievement" refers to standardized test scores. Policymakers financially reward achievement, and punish schools that do not make progress based on this standard. Is the movement toward "accountability" hurting or helping schools?

LEGISLATED ACCOUNTABILITY

No Child Left Behind

In the context of the elementary school, accountability refers to holding teachers, administrators, schools, and districts responsible for students' academic outcomes. It certainly is a complicated issue. With so many stakeholders demanding proof of success of our schools, a variety of accountability measures have been developed. The major starting point for accountability in the United States was a federal law known as the No Child Left Behind Act (NCLB) that went into effect under the Bush administration in 2002. Among other things, the law required annual testing in all states to measure student performance. The tests and accountability measures differed from state-to-state. North Carolina implemented a school-based management and accountability program called *The ABC's of Education*, and the tests were often referred to as EOGs (end of grade) or EOCs (end of course). Decisions on school funding and programs were largely determined by the results of these tests. Although there was some variability between states, students were mandatorily tested in reading, math, writing, and science beginning in the third grade. NCLB decisions for elementary schools were made based on the performance of these third through fifth graders. Schools that do met goals for performance and growth were awarded stipends for success. Schools that continually failed to meet goals for progress were forced to accept intervention teams from the state to work for improvement. Such programs provided much needed money for schools, but linked it directly to achievement and growth.

According to NCLB, each state was charged with developing and implementing a system of accountability designed to ensure that all schools made *Adequate Yearly Progress* (AYP). In order to make AYP, schools had to meet the following objectives:

- High standards of academic achievement for all (largely based on a standardized test score): For example, a standardized test is scored 1 to 5, and the school gets points for every student that scores 3 or above.
- Continuous and substantial academic improvement for all students: For example, the school gets points for every student that improves from a 1 or 2 the previous year to a 3 or above the present year.

- Separate measureable annual objectives for all students and the following subgroups:
  - All students
  - Different racial/ethnic groups
  - Low-income students
  - Students with disabilities
  - Students with Limited English Proficiency (LEP)

A system of sanctions and rewards was based on student achievement. Importantly, this model of accountability included achievement for *all* students. Specific attention had to be paid to traditionally underserved populations (including children with disabilities, from low-income families, non-English speakers, as well as African-Americans and Latinos), as these groups were required to show progress separately from the progress of all students.

MINI-SCENARIO (In teachers' lounge):

Ms. Johnson (new teacher): In math, I am supposed to be teaching area, but I have a lot of kids who still do not know how to multiply. I don't know what to do.

Ms. Robinson (experienced teacher): I know what you mean, only 3 or 4 of my students are reading at grade level. The problem is we have to stick to the curriculum as written.

Ms. Johnson: I can't. How can they realistically learn area without knowing how to multiply?

Ms. Robinson: You have to. Area is on the state test, and that is how the students are evaluated... come to think of it, that is how WE are evaluated. Anything not on the curriculum, you will have to do with your door closed.

Ms. Johnson: With my door closed?

Opportunity *for* dialogue:

Think about the dilemma this new teacher is facing. What does Ms. Robinson mean when she says "with your door closed?"

Schools that made AYP were financially rewarded. Oftentimes this money was utilized to supplement teacher salaries. Schools that did not make AYP for consecutive years were required to implement and document **school improvement plans** in consultation with administration, teachers, parents, staff, district, and outside consultants. After a year, the school was mandated to provide academic assistance, including supplemental educational services (usually tutoring programs), and public school choice. Schools had to purchase textbooks and other learning materials that had been approved by the federal government. These schools were then audited to ensure that teachers are strictly following the instructions in the programs. If they were in violation, they could lose funding. Principals in ineffective schools could be fired, teachers could be stripped of their tenure and fired, and students could be held back. After multiple years, the school must implement **corrective action.**

After multiple years of not making AYP, the school had to develop and implement the SIP *and* at least one of the following:

- Replace staff
- Revise curriculum
- Decrease management authority
- Appoint outside advisors
- Extend the school year or school day
- Completely restructure

If corrective action fails, the state may take over the school or enter into a contract with a private/charter entity.

MINI-SCENARIO (staff meeting):

Ms. Hunter (principal): Last year, our state reading test scores were in the twentieth percentile. The district is looking for a 10% increase. For the next few weeks we will be using these test practice workbooks.

Ms. Robinson: You want us to teach to the test?

Ms. Hunter: I want you to teach the skills the students need.

Mr. Lam (P.E. Teacher): Why do I have a set of books?

Ms. Hunter: For the time being, ALL teachers will devote time to teaching Reading sample questions.

Ms. Johnson (to Ms. Robinson): If we teach the test questions, what are we really assessing?

Ms. Robinson (to Ms. Johnson): It assesses us. The test scores go up, they can say the schools are improving; the scores stay down, they can't.

Race to the Top

In 2009, the Obama administration introduced a new accountability measure known as Race to the Top (RTTT). This initiative set aside over 4 billion dollars of federal education funds, for which states can compete. The goal was to stimulate innovative methods of reform. To apply for these funds, states were asked to provide evidence of positive reform in five specific areas: (a) design and implementation of quality standards and assessments, (b) supporting effective data systems with a goal of improving instruction, (c) recruitment and retention of effective teachers and principals, (d) improving performance in the lowest-achieving schools, (e) providing a model for sustaining effective reform. States (including North Carolina) have been awarded funds as a result of RTTT, whereas four states did not apply. North Carolina was awarded $400 million.

NORTH CAROLINA'S PATH POST-NCLB

In early 2012, the Obama Administration passed a provision allowing states to opt-out of NCLB requirements. In part because under 30% of North Carolina's public schools were making AYP according to NCLB requirements, North Carolina was one of the states that applied for and received waiver approval. In order to receive a waiver, states agreed to implement their own accountability plans. The legislation requires that the state-developed plans involve college and career preparation, a focus on the neediest students, and support for effective teaching and leadership. Many of the state plans developed thus far closely mirror the accountability requirements of NCLB (albeit without the federal AYP designations) and revolve around state testing. A major part of North Carolina's plan, the addition of a system to evaluate teacher success based on student test scores, is discussed in Chapter 8. Beginning in 2013, the NC began using student test scores as a means to assign a letter grade to each school (as part of the NC School Report Card plan). These grades are assigned to every public school based largely on average test performance of 3rd - 5th graders. At the writing of this book, there is a policy proposal on the table which would lessen the amount of required testing in schools. However, presently elementary schools require EOGs in Reading, Math and Science, in addition to practice tests throughout the year.

A DIFFERENT LOOK AT "ACCOUNTABILITY":

State and federal accountability measures have increased test scores, raised measurable standards, and provided detailed reports on student test performance to government, schools, teachers, and parents. Specific attention is now paid to traditionally underperforming and underserved populations. As a result, teachers have been cited as being more accountable for student success. In some cases throughout the country, reward money is paid to schools and teachers that meet standards for all groups, and supplemental tutoring services are provided for schools that do not. As well-meaning as many of these accountability programs might have been, it appears that in some cases they have missed the mark. The focus in many schools quickly shifted to the test scores and preparing children to pass the tests. Schools increased the time spent in tested subjects, mainly reading, math, and writing, and other subjects began to be slighted. School leaders have been heard to say, "Spend your time on the tested subjects, don't worry about social studies this week," or "Let's prepare for the tests. That is what we will be judged by."

Let us return to these questions asked in Chapter 1:

- What happened to recesses?
- What happened to field trips?
- What happened to time to talk with students and for students to talk with each other?
- What happened to the fun in school?
- What happened to spring festivals, winter carnivals, plays, and assemblies?
- What happened to inquiry and to exploring our questions about the world?
- What happened to authentic learning?
- What happened to time to learn not just go through the motions?

Test-based accountability measures have met much opposition with teachers and policymakers. Opponents argue that, (a) mandated curriculum assigned to schools "in need of improvement" often have trivial requirements, and are script-based, detracting from the creative abilities of our incredible teachers, (b) the laws have led to an unbalanced focus on test practice material, especially in low-performing elementary schools serving minority students, and (c) test-practice protocols have lead to the marginalization of untested subjects such as social studies and the fine arts. Schools sacrificing art, music, physical education, social studies, science, and even lunch and recess are most likely to be those that serve "low-performing subgroups." Education tends to look different for these students.

State-mandated tutoring and curriculum programs assigned to schools that do not make the grade are often designed for test-preparation, and are often characterized by fact memorization and prepackaged scripted lesson plans. What impact may this have on student interest? What impact may practice testing have on true instructional time? To be sure, a higher number of teachers in schools housing "low-performing subgroups" will report that test preparation-based lessons are required and monitored. What is the specific influence on these populations of students?

Besides the rigors of standardized testing, teachers are accountable to their students in several ways. You will be accountable for keeping your students safe (both physically and emotionally), you will be accountable for teaching and learning, you will be accountable for making a connection with your students, and you will be accountable for putting smiles on their faces. This is the incredible work of an elementary teacher.

ELEMENTARY PROGRAMS AND PRACTICES
EDN 300
OPPORTUNITY FOR DEBATE:
PROS AND CONS OF STANDARDIZED TEST-BASED ACCOUNTABILITY

Name:

Pros	Cons

ELEMENTARY PROGRAMS AND PRACTICES
EDN 300
OPPORTUNITY FOR DIALOGUE

Name:

Chapter:

CHAPTER seven
Effective Planning

"He who opens a school door, closes a prison.

– Victor Hugo

What connections can you make with this statement by Victor Hugo?

When we think about the incredible work that we do in the elementary school, there is really no excuse for not being prepared. Every student deserves to be in a classroom where the teacher is always prepared and where they are invited into professional, effective, and exciting learning experiences. Most teachers can share stories of staying up late into the night, getting up at 4 a.m., or working on the weekends to ensure that they are prepared and that the students will have meaningful engagements for the next day. This also includes timely and significant feedback. This is what we do as teachers.

> My first principal told us of his very first day of teaching. He had worked hard to set up his classroom. He had worked hard to be prepared for that important first day with his students. He was excited. He was anxious. He was very nervous. He knew he was prepared—he knew what he wanted to do. He said the children came in and he began the day, following his plans. By 10:45 that morning, he had done everything he had planned. We asked him what he did then. He said he started at the beginning and did it all again.

Needless to say, preparation is paramount to effective teaching. In this chapter we will explore the benefits of being prepared and some information that might be useful in doing effective planning for our classrooms.

WHAT IS A LESSON PLAN?

When many people think of planning, they think of lesson plans. While lesson plans can be an important tool in our planning and while many principals require lesson plans be prepared and submitted for approval, it is important to keep lesson plans in their proper place. They are simply a tool for helping us be prepared. I think it is actually possible to have a wonderful lesson plan but not really be prepared to teach. I think it is actually possible to focus so much on the lesson plan that we lose sight of our students and their needs as well as opportunities to enhance the learning of our students.

What a Lesson Plan Is	What a Lesson Plan Isn't
A template for planning	The most important part of the process
A structure for thinking	Something we can find on the Internet to cut down on time
A starting point for our learning engagements	Something to be followed without any variation
Structure to help us think about our students and plan specific learning engagements to help them	Something we can get off the Internet without even thinking about our students and their specific needs
Focused on learning	Focused on activities
Something that takes effort to create to ensure it is useful and meaningful	Something to quickly get done so we can go home early

As we begin the planning process, it can be helpful to have a template to help ensure that we don't leave out any of the important aspects of our planning. You will probably see a variety of lesson plan structures. The main points of some popular lesson plans are explained below:

SIX POINT LESSON PLAN

This is a very traditional format for a lesson plan that is widely used. It is typical of the lesson plans found in many classrooms and schools.

Focus and Review. As we begin a lesson, we might ask ourselves what can be done to help our students focus on the topic for the lesson? Is there an exciting way to invite them into the learning? It can be helpful to review what was covered in a previous engagement in order to help students begin to make connections with the topic of this engagement. Helping students know what the lesson will be about can also be supportive of learning.

Statement of Objective. This is the opportunity for us to articulate clearly what we want students to learn or be able to do as a result of this lesson. Once we state a clear objective, we know where we are headed and we know what to look for in order to determine if we were successful in helping our students get there.

Teacher Input. This is the part of the lesson where we instruct—where we provide specific information, present concepts, demonstrate procedures, or give specific feedback.

Guided Practice. This allows students the opportunity to practice the skill or use of the concept while the teacher is there to guide and show the way. This might include having the students do one problem, then show them the answer and the way the problem was solved. It might include having a child read, then being there to help them be successful with the reading or use of a strategy.

Independent Practice. This is an opportunity for students to practice on their own. Often this is done as homework.

Closure. This is the way to bring the lesson to an end. It is an opportunity to summarize what was learned, review a process, and help students make connections that are so important to learning. This is also an opportunity to assess the success of the lesson. Did students reach the objective? Was the lesson structure effective? What should be changed to ensure a better engagement? Where are the students and, based on that, what would next best steps be?

FIVE E'S

This lesson plan format might be helpful in a more constructivist classroom.

Engage. What can I do to engage the students, to pique their interest, to help them understand what learning in the area can do for them? What invitations can be offered to bring students into the learning opportunities that are part of this lesson? What decisions must students make?

Explore. What can best help students be able to explore their topic? How might students go about their exploration? What materials, manipulatives, demonstrations, etc. would be helpful? What questions might students ask? How much time might be required for this to happen?

Explain. What structures would best support students in explaining what they have learned? How might the teacher demonstrate processes or help highlight significant concepts?

Elaborate. How can the teacher best support students in articulating what they learned and elaborating on it—extending their understanding, generating additional questions, choosing to explore more deeply, discussing with other students, etc.?

Evaluate. In what ways can the teacher evaluate what was learned and how successful the engagement was? In what ways can students evaluate what they learned and the processes and strategies they used in their learning?

INQUIRY

As the name implies, this structure might be useful in an inquiry lesson.

Objective. What are we trying to accomplish? What do we hope students will be able to do as a result of this learning engagement? What is the focus of our inquiry?

Prerequisite Knowledge. Is there any knowledge that would be essential for successful inquiry in this area? If so, what is it and how is it best presented? How can the teacher know if students have this essential knowledge?

Materials Needed. What is needed in order for this inquiry to be successful and productive? How best should it be provided? Is there enough?

Question. Is there a question, or questions, that should guide our inquiry? How can the teacher best support students in generating important questions? Will the questions stimulate inquiry?

Prediction. What outcomes and/or learning will students predict? How can the teacher best support students in making predictions that will help guide and focus our inquiry?

Investigation. How might students conduct their investigation? What do students need to know in order to conduct a successful investigation? How can the teacher best support the investigation?

Conclusions Reached. What was the result of the investigation? What conclusions and connections will students be able to make? How can feedback best be given?

Evaluation. How can the teacher assess what was learned and the progress of students in this area? What should be assessed? How can students assess what they learned and how they are growing?

As you can see, there is a wide range of possible lesson plan structures from which to choose. Can you see similarities with all of these lesson plan structures? What major points do they all include? How are they different? Teachers typically develop a system that works best for them. The format is not the most important aspect of our planning. That said, it is important to note that it is easier to plan from a specific philosophical perspective using one lesson plan format than it might be with another one.

Opportunity *for* dialogue:

Can you see why a particular lesson plan format might fit better with one philosophy than another? What philosophical perspective would best fit with the six point lesson plan format? What about a constructivist perspective? Can you see how a teacher's philosophy will determine the questions they ask, the kinds of engagements they create, and the ways in which they support learning?

BENEFITS OF PLANNING

In addition to the fact that we owe it to our students to plan effectively—to be prepared for every lesson and to be organized, there are many benefits to effective planning.

- We have a better chance for success.

    We will have done the thinking and the preparation necessary for success. We will know where we are going and how to tell when we get there. We will have all materials ready. We will know the content we are trying to help students learn. We will know it well enough to engender passion. We will be able to help students make the connections that are essential for learning to happen. We will have thought through the flow of the lesson, looking for possible problems and opportunities.

- We will be more confident.

  Effective planning allows us to relax and not be stressed. We have everything ready, we know what we will be doing, where we will be stationed, and what we will be looking for.

- Planning helps with classroom management.

  Students know when we aren't prepared. They can sense it. Unpreparedness can spawn numerous classroom management challenges.

- Planning helps us create needed structure.

  Planning can help us come to know structures that should be in place to support learning. It will allow us the opportunity to ensure those structures are in place.

- We can better provide consistency and security.

  One way to help support learning and create an environment that is inviting and conducive to learning, is to provide consistency. When students know what to expect and how the classroom operates, it also provides security for them. They are more willing to take the risks that are essential for learning to happen.

- Planning allows us to be flexible.

  When we are well prepared and know what we are trying to accomplish, it allows us to be more flexible. We don't have to rely on a script. We can be about the business of truly supporting the learning of our students. We can truly teach.

- Planning enables us to empower our students.

  I'm not sure how we can empower our students as learners if we don't plan to do so.

- We are able to become kid watchers.

  Planning allows us to get away from the lesson plan and the details of the lesson, and truly be able to watch our students. We are better able to support their learning because we can watch them in action. We can observe the process.

- Planning allows us to differentiate our instruction.

  Part of our planning should include how to meet the needs of each student in our classrooms. We are not able to differentiate our instruction unless we have taken the time to plan and to think about each child.

- We are able to follow teachable moments.

  When we are prepared, we have thought about possible eventualities and are able to take advantage of teachable moments that always seem to come up in a lesson. If we are not confident, if we are not well-prepared, we will be less willing to deviate from the lesson plan to follow student interests, questions, or other important teachable moments.

Opportunity *for* **dialogue:** What other advantages can you see for effective planning?

PLANNING—A STRUCTURE FOR THINKING

It can be helpful to view planning as an opportunity to think. We want to think through every aspect of the lesson so we are as prepared as possible for anything that could happen during the lesson. Some questions that might guide our planning could include:

- What am I trying to accomplish?
- What do I want to have happen?
- How will it look?
- What materials will I need?
- How will I know if I get there?
- How can I best assess?
- What questions should I ask?
- What questions might students ask?
- How can I stimulate discussion?
- How can I let go? Provide ownership?
- What opportunities can I see to empower my learners?
- What demonstrations are needed?
- What questions might they ask?
- What should I do if we finish early?
- What should I do if we need more time?
- What are some teachable moments that might come up?
- What are some possible hurdles that might materialize?
- Have I done what I am asking students to do?
- Who needs what?
- What is the flow of the lesson? What logistics do I need to be aware of?
- Where should I position myself?
- What will I look for?
- What is my focus today or during this time?

Opportunity *for* **dialogue:** What other questions can you think of? Can you see how planning is really an opportunity to think? Pick a couple of questions and identify how they would help us be better prepared to teach.

SOME COMMON PLANNING PITFALLS

Knowing some of the common pitfalls in planning can help us do a better job with our thinking and preparation. Oft times these become pitfalls because we fail to think about them. Some of the pitfalls to avoid in planning would include the following:

- How can we best distribute materials?
    When should we do it? Before the lesson? After we have explained the engagement?

How should we do it?

What materials are needed?

Is there a way to prepare materials so they can be distributed more efficiently?

- Are there other logistics we need to be aware of?

Where are materials located? Can they be accessed by the students?

Is there space to put projects when students are finished?

Can students get around the room as needed?

Are desks and tables organized to support the kind of engagement planned?

- Do we know our students as learners?

What do they know already?

What are they able to accomplish?

What are their strengths upon which we can build?

- Do we have a firm grasp of the content we are presenting?

Do we know it well enough to answer questions?

Can we help our students make connections to other things they have learned?

Are we prepared to help students generate their own questions?

Have we made notes in our lesson plans to help us with the content as needed?

- Do we have a well-defined objective? Is it measureable?

The student will be able to…

- Have we thought about what the lesson entails?

How much time will it take?

Do we have the amount of time we need?

What skills will be required for students to be successful? Do they have them?

What are some of the connections we hope students will be able to make?

- Have we thought through possible scenarios?

Have we identified "What if's?" What if this happens? What if this doesn't happen?

Have we identified what our students will be doing while we work with other students?

Have we thought about where we should position ourselves in order to do what we need to do?

- Have we identified the demonstrations we need to set and prepared to ensure that they happen?

What demonstration would be beneficial?

How can we best show them?

- Are we focused on the plan or on the learning?
- Are we focused on learning or on activities?

A group of interns was discussing the amount of time they spend making lesson plans for their teaching. One student said it was taking hours to get good lesson plans ready. Another student said that she simply goes online to a couple of lesson plan sites, finds one that seems to work and downloads it. She said, "It only takes me about 15 minutes to get all of my lesson plans ready. Then I have time to myself.

Opportunity *for* dialogue:

What are the pros and cons of each of these positions? If you knew of a teacher or colleague who was planning this way, what advice would you give them?

It can be very helpful to keep the big picture in mind as we plan. If we are planning against the backdrop of what we are trying to accomplish in the long period, it will help ensure that we are moving toward our goals. For example, before I began to do any planning for the year, I established some overarching goals that I wanted to accomplish. My reading goals might be:

To create students who can read, who do read, and who enjoy reading.
To create proficient readers who:

- Have confidence in their abilities to read and learn
- Are independent readers
- Are effective problem solvers
- Have an impressive repertoire of strategies to use while reading
- Comprehend and create knowledge as they read
- Have a healthy understanding of the reading process and can discuss what happens as they read
- Use reading to change their lives for the better

The next step for me was to identify the strategies and engagements that were essential to my ability to meet the goals that I had set. I felt it was essential to demonstrate reading strategies and provide opportunities to practice the strategies, introduce exciting books and authors, have effective literature response groups, have significant time for writing, create an effective silent reading program, and take time to read aloud to students every day.

The next thing I did was to organize my weekly schedule. I determined how much time I needed for each engagement. I listed all of the things that I wanted to do each week in my classroom. I determined the engagements that were "musts" in my classroom—the ones that I absolutely needed to have in order to meet the goals I had set. Once my weekly schedule was set, it became an easier task to do my more specific planning. My weekly schedule looked as follows. I have gone into specific detail in the language arts block to demonstrate this point. These are the engagements and structures that I absolutely need in order to meet my goals.

My Schedule

Time	Monday	Tuesday	Wednesday	Thursday	Friday
8:00-9:00	Math	Math	Math	Math	Math
9:00-9:30	Art/Music	Art/Music	Art/Music	Art/Music	Art/Music
9:30-9:45	Recess	Recess	Recess	Recess	Recess
9:45-10:15	Reading Strategy	Choral Reading	Reading Strategy	Choral Reading	Reading Strategy
10:15-10:45	Lit Response	Book Intro	Lit Response	Author Intro	Lit Response
10:45-11:30	Writing	Writing	Writing	Writing	Writing
11:30-11:45	Oral Reading	Oral Reading	Oral Reading	Oral Reading	Oral Reading
11:45-12:30	Lunch	Lunch	Lunch	Lunch	Lunch
12:30-1:00	DEAR	DEAR	DEAR	DEAR	DEAR
1:00-1:45	Social Studies	Social Studies	Social Studies	Science	Science
1:45-2:45	PE	PE	PE	PE	PE
2:45-3:00	Closing	Closing	Closing	Closing	Closing

To continue with the discussion about planning, let's look specifically at the time between 9:45 and 11:45. Here is what it looks like:

9:45-10:15	Reading Strategy	Choral Reading	Reading Strategy	Choral Reading	Reading Strategy
10:15-10:45	Lit Response	Book Intro	Lit Response	Author Intro	Lit Response
10:45-11:30	Writing	Writing	Writing	Writing	Writing
11:30-11:45	Oral Reading	Oral Reading	Oral Reading	Oral Reading	Oral Reading

Now, as I plan for the coming week, I can use the template I have created to help focus my thinking. For example, I know that on Monday, Wednesday, and Friday, I need to be prepared to present a reading strategy. The best way to determine what strategy I want to cover is to watch my students. I have determined that my students could benefit from some discussion and demonstration of the strategy, "When you are reading and you come to something you don't know, it can be helpful to ask, 'what should the word be?'" This might be a way to help us as we read. So, I think through the best ways to help students learn that strategy. I have decided that on Monday we will use a passage from the book we are reading aloud to provide some context for our learning. We read this page two days ago. I will read page 17 and share the strategy with the students. On Wednesday, I will use a pen pal letter that one of our students received and have the students read it as a class. There are some words in the letter that we could not identify so this will be good practice for the strategy. I will also ask the students to put sticky notes in their reading books when they come to something they don't know and use the new strategy we have introduced. On Friday, I will ask students to share an example of how they used the strategy.

I also know that I must have two selections ready for our Choral Reading experience. I have chosen to use the poem "Sick," by Shel Silverstein on Tuesday and

I have chosen to have a "requests day" for Thursday. This means that the students can request any poem or other choral reading we have done in the past.

Likewise, I know that I need to prepare for the three days of literature response groups. I know that I can't get to all six groups every day but I can get to them every week. Therefore, I plan to go to the groups that need me that day. I know where the groups are with their reading. I think about each student in the group and prepare by thinking about strategies I can highlight, comments I want to make about the books they are reading, etc. I have reserved Fridays for my time to read with students one on one and do assessment conferences. I have listed the names of the students I will meet with on Friday. Each child has a folder with notes about progress. I review those folders, making notes of things to highlight, questions to ask, etc. In preparation for author introduction, I gather material to use in that presentation. This week, I have determined to introduce the book, *A Year Down Yonder* by Richard Peck. It is such a great book. I will identify a few short passages to read to the class to try to "hook" them on the book. On Thursday, I plan to introduce Gary Paulsen because I would like to use one of his books as a read aloud as we finish the current book. Here again, I have gathered material needed to present a solid introduction of this wonderful author.

During the writing workshop time, I prepare by identifying students who need a writing conference, who are ready for author's circle, and who have written something that I think would be of benefit for the whole class and help me in demonstrating effective writing strategies. I also identify specific topics for mini-lessons used to help students with their writing.

I feel it is essential that I read aloud to students every day. During this time, we are currently reading one of my favorite books, *Summer of the Monkeys* by Wilson Rawls, I prepare by reading the two chapters I plan to read each day so that I remember the story and am prepared for things that might come up in the book.

The detailed weekly schedule might look like this:

9:45-10:15	Reading Strategy What should the word be? Use pg 17 of *Summer of the Monkeys*	Choral Reading "Sick" by Shel Silverstein	Reading Strategy What should the word be? Use Pen pal letter	Choral Reading-Request day	Reading Strategy What should the word be? Students share an instance when they used the strategy
10:15-10:30	Lit Response Grp 1: Focus on development of character Grp 4: Reciprocal Teaching after chap 6 Grp 5: Sharing activity	Book Intro *A Year Down Yonder*; Read pg 25-26; Give overview of book: Spending time with grandma—How about a year? Discuss Grandma Dowdel	Lit Response Grp 2: Inference. How did you know Snape was evil? Grp 3: Lit circles grooming Grp 6: Flashback technique with Paul Mather	Author Intro Gary Paulsen Trumpet club video; Highlight of his life; 1st library card; reading like a wolf eats; trapping and dog team; Other books: *Hatchet, Dog Song, The Voyage of the Frog*	Lit Response Miscue Analysis: John Eric Kathy Katie Brian (Here I have chosen to spend this time with the above named students in assessment) I will read with each one, doing a Miscue Analysis
10:45-11:00	Writer's Workshop <u>Writing Conf:</u> Brad, Greg, Wes, Ann <u>Author's Circle:</u> Tiffany Stephanie <u>Share:</u> Kevin, Brian, Laura, Emily	Writer's Workshop <u>Writing Conf:</u> <u>Author's Circle:</u> <u>Share:</u> <u>Mini-Lesson:</u> Revising	Writer's Workshop <u>Writing Conf:</u> <u>Author's Circle:</u> <u>Share:</u> <u>Mini-Lesson:</u> Revising	Writer's Workshop <u>Writing Conf:</u> <u>Author's Circle</u> <u>Share:</u> <u>Mini-Lesson:</u> Good beginnings	Writer's Workshop <u>Writing Conf:</u> <u>Author's Circle:</u> <u>Share:</u> <u>Mini-Lesson:</u> Good beginnings
11:30-11:45	Oral Reading *Summer of the Monkeys* Ch 8-9	Oral Reading *Summer of the Monkeys* Ch 10-11	Oral Reading *Summer of the Monkeys* Ch 12-13	Oral Reading *Summer of the Monkeys* Ch 14-15	Oral Reading *Summer of the Monkeys* Ch 16-17

SUMMARY

Planning is an essential part of our craft. It is one more key to the incredible work of the elementary school. As we hone our skills in planning, we will be more and more effective in supporting the learning of our students. Someone has said that if we fail to plan, we plan to fail. We simply cannot be lax with our planning. Our students deserve more and we owe it to ourselves to be well-prepared.

ELEMENTARY PROGRAMS AND PRACTICES
EDN 300
OPPORTUNITY FOR DIALOGUE

Name:

Chapter:

CHAPTER eight
Teaching Standards

" I cannot teach anybody anything, I can only make them think.

– Socrates "

Think of your favorite elementary school teacher. List the qualities that made him or her a great teacher.

As you read this chapter, let's compare the qualities you have listed with the standards put forth by State and National entities to define a successful teacher. What similarities can you find? How does your list differ?

EDUCATIVE TEACHER PERFORMANCE ASSESSMENT (EDTPA)

The first set of teaching standards you will have to meet on your journey to become an elementary teacher will be during your teacher preparation program. You will be asked to demonstrate that your proficiency as an educator in order to qualify for your state's teaching license. In North Carolina (and most other states) you will have to meet the standards put forth by edTPA.

edTPA is a performance-based assessment developed by educators for educators, and is the first such assessment to be nationally available. It involves a rigorous process that requires teacher candidates to demonstrate that they meet certain standards and have the classroom skills necessary to ensure students are learning. Detailed information can be found at http://edtpa.aacte.org/about-edtpa.

At the elementary level, this involves meeting standards in three important areas: planning, instruction, and assessment. First, teacher candidates must develop a learning segment and provide research-based commentary that explains all of the instructional choices made within their lesson plans. Then, teacher candidates will record themselves teaching the learning segment, and provide written rationale for choices made during instruction. Lastly, teacher candidates will collect and analyze student work, and provide commentary on the assessment and feedback process. edTPA doesn't ask you to do anything that you aren't already doing in your preparation programs, but it does ask for greater rationale for and demonstration of these essential skills.

NORTH CAROLINA PROFESSIONAL TEACHING STANDARDS (NCPTS)

Like those in many states throughout the nation, the North Carolina State Board of Education has defined their mission as preparing students for life in the 21st Century. The North Carolina Professional Teaching Standards Commission has defined the following as the standards teachers must meet to be successful:

1. Teachers demonstrate leadership.

In addition to setting a positive example as a role-model for your students, this standard also encompasses demonstrating leadership in the school and in the profession. In the classroom this means a teacher is expected to empower students and take responsibility for both their successes and failures. Being a leader involves collaboration with colleagues, and a constant striving for professional growth. Most importantly, a teacher who is a leader creates a safe environment for their students.

Is this a quality that you recognized in your favorite elementary school teacher? Was the classroom organized and under control? Did he or she help you when you needed help and praise you when you did good work?

2. Teachers establish a respectful environment for a diverse population of students.

A diverse population of students includes differences in school readiness, differences in race or ethnicity, differences in gender, differences in socioeconomic status, differences in culture, etc. *Establishing a respectful environment* for your students means acknowledging these differences as beneficial to your classroom environment, and not as detrimental. It means being inclusive and adapting to all of your students' needs. It means treating your students as individuals, building relationships with your students and their families, and counteracting negative stereotypes or preconceived notions. Instructionally, this means incorporating histories and contributions of all cultures, different points of view, and recognizing that a student's various identities may influence their performance.

Opportunity *for* dialogue: What are some topics in elementary school social studies instruction, where this standard may particularly apply?

Some instructional topics where embracing diversity may directly apply in elementary school social studies include teaching immigration, faith-based holidays, slavery, segregation, and Columbus Day. Of course, there are several others. To demonstrate successfully meeting this standard, let's use the teaching of Columbus Day as an example:

What is traditionally taught to elementary students regarding Columbus Day?
- Christopher Columbus discovered America in 1492
- The Nina, the Pinta, and the Santa Maria
- Columbus was from Italy, but financed by the King and Queen of Spain to find spices and gold
- Most believed Earth was flat, Columbus set out to prove it was round
- Columbus discovered America
- Columbus thought he was near India, and called natives "Indians"

What else do we know historically?
- Christopher Columbus did not "discover" America, many reached the "New World" before him

- In 1492, many people believed the Earth to be round
- Columbus enslaved Native Americans for profit
- Millions of Native Americans died from disease and murder by the new settlers

  •

Most Native American students are probably aware of the latter facts. The tendency, however, is for teachers to teach as we have been taught. If you had Native American students in your class, how would you sensitively include their stories to meet standard 2 and maintain a respectful learning environment for all?

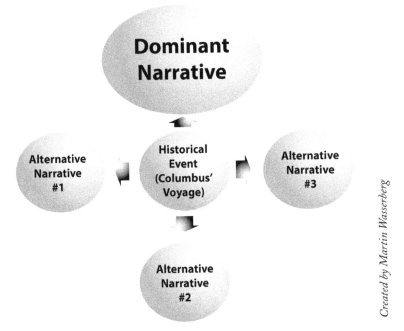

Created by Martin Wasserberg

The goal of teaching inclusively is not to eliminate and replace the dominant narrative, but to recognize different narratives; in our example, that of Native Americans.

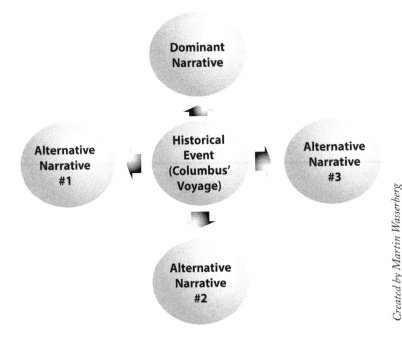

Created by Martin Wasserberg

INCLUSIVE TEACHING

An example of teaching Columbus Day in a culturally-inclusive manner in an elementary school classroom may look like this:

- First, imagine you are a sailor travelling across the ocean on Columbus' first journey. Describe what happens when you finally reach land.
- Now, imagine you are a Native American living when Columbus first reaches shore. Describe what happens when his crew finally reaches land.

Here, students are required to evaluate history from different perspectives, without presenting one as more important than another.

3. Teachers know the content they teach.

Simply put, teachers should know their stuff! In a classroom, this includes aligning your lesson plans with the state and national standards (not just "winging it"). In order to do so, a successful teacher should know what his or her students were expected to learn the previous years, and build upon that, and also be aware of what is on the horizon. For example, if students learned how to find the area of a rectangle last year, that may be a good place to start before moving to irregular figures. Also, if a teacher knows that next year students will be expected to know how to calculate the area of a circle, a little preview may be in order this year.

Knowing the state and national standards also should facilitate the ability of teachers to relate content across disciplines. Using *Cloudy with a Chance of Meatballs* to teach about adjectives? Why not coordinate that with a weather lesson in science? Teaching weather in science? Why not coordinate that with temperature in math? Recognizing how disciplines are interconnected and relating content across the curriculum in this manner allows for your students to make those same connections, and increases opportunities for comprehension.

Most importantly, a teacher who knows their content must also know how to make this content relevant to their students. For example, a child who has never been to a farm may have more trouble comprehending *Charlotte's Web* than a child who lives on a farm. It is the responsibility of the teacher to provide experiences and background knowledge to make new instruction relevant to those children. With the plethora of resources available in the 21st Century with the click of a mouse, there is no excuse for leaving such children behind.

Opportunity *for* dialogue:

How might a lesson about seasons look for kindergarteners:
a) In Miami, FL
b) In Wilmington, NC
c) In Anchorage, Alaska
d) In New York City

4. Teachers facilitate learning for their students.

In addition to knowing *what* students should learn, successful teachers also know *how* their students learn. Successful teachers understand that their students are individuals who each learn differently, and plan their instruction accordingly. In the classroom, this means using a variety of teaching methods and materials at grade level, and navigating between them as appropriate. For example, successful teachers know when group work is appropriate, know how to meaningfully integrate technology, and know when a teacher-directed lesson is necessary. That is, they *differentiate* their instruction to adapt to the learning needs of their students.

A fourth grade classroom in which a teacher has successfully differentiated instruction may look like this:

- Mr. Marks works with six students at the back table. He is presenting a small teacher-directed lesson on reducing fractions to students who did not fair too well on the previous assessment. Another group of six students is experimenting with fraction bars, recording different ways of expressing the same fraction on a worksheet that Mr. Marks had developed beforehand. Four students are on the computer exploring the fractions lesson on a school-provided math program, while four others are competing in a fraction flash card activity. Do you remember anything similar from your favorite elementary school teacher?

Opportunity *for* dialogue:

How is the above classroom meeting Standard #4 as delineated in the NCPTS document?

5. Teachers reflect on their practice.

Becoming a successful teacher is a never-ending process. Each year you will receive a different group of students, with different needs and different experiences. In this regard, constant reflection is of the utmost importance. Successful teachers are always ready and willing to incorporate new ideas, and lessons learned from professional development and collaborating with colleagues.

Mini-Scenario

Mrs. James has been teaching 20 years, and is taken off-guard when the assistant principal discusses her less than perfect annual observation with her.

Assistant Principal: It seemed that the students were not engaged. I did not see any evidence of learning.

Ms. James: I don't understand. I have been teaching the same lessons for 20 years.

Assistant Principal: Maybe that is the problem.

Successful teachers constantly analyze their students' learning and are able to determine what they are teaching well, and what can be improved.

6. Teachers contribute to the academic success of their students.

Beginning in the 2012-2013 school year, North Carolina developed a new state-based accountability system and was granted federal permission to opt out of many NCLB requirements. A major part of this new accountability system included the addition of Standard 6 to the NCPTS. Academic success, in terms of this standard, is defined by student test scores. Teachers are to be evaluated based on a three-year rolling average of student growth.

NATIONAL BOARD FOR PROFESSIONAL TEACHING STANDARDS (NBPTS)

The NBPTS was created in 1987, answering a call to prepare teachers for the 21st Century. The Board put forth five core propositions which they believed characterized successful teachers. The propositions are listed below, with narrative on how they relate to the NCPTS:

Proposition 1: Teachers are committed to students and their learning.
This proposition indicates a belief that all students can learn. It encompasses what is discussed in North Carolina Professional Teaching Standard 2 above, but goes beyond in putting forth that successful teachers are characterized by a *commitment* to the profession. It is this commitment that should drive teachers to meet these standards.

Proposition 2: Teachers know the subjects they teach and how to teach those subjects to students.
This proposition is a combination of North Carolina Professional Teaching Standards 3 and 4. Great teachers not only know the content, but know how to best deliver it to their specific population of students.

Proposition 3: Teachers are responsible for managing and monitoring student learning.
Taking responsibility for both student successes and failures is part of being a leader in the classroom. This proposition is a combination of NCPTS 1 and NCPTS 4. According to the National Board for Professional Teaching Standards, part of being a teacher-leader is differentiating instruction to meet the instructional and motivational needs of one's students.

Proposition 4: Teachers think systematically about their practice and learn from experience.
Proposition 4 mirrors NCPTS 5. The National Board for Professional Teaching

Standards believes successful teachers not only critically examine their practices, but constantly research and stay aware of current issues in education

Proposition 5: Teachers are members of learning communities.
NCPTS 1 indicates that being a leader involves collaboration with colleagues. The National Board Standards expand upon this idea by stating that successful teachers are invariably members of learning communities. These learning communities could include grade level colleagues, community agencies, and/or other professionals with a goal of improving student learning.

The NBPTS goes beyond an overarching list of core propositions for all students. In addition, specific standards are listed for each subject area in which one can receive National Board Certification. The following are the standards most relevant to elementary education:

Early Childhood/Generalist Standards (3-8):

1. Understanding young children
2. Equity, fairness, and diversity
3. Assessment
4. Promoting child development and learning
5. Knowledge of integrated curriculum
6. Multiple teaching strategies for meaningful learning
7. Family and community partnerships
8. Professional partnerships
9. Reflective practice

Middle Childhood/Generalist Standards (7-12):

1. Knowledge of students
2. Knowledge of content and curriculum
3. Learning environment
4. Respect for diversity
5. Instructional resources
6. Meaningful applications of knowledge
7. Multiple paths to knowledge
8. Assessment
9. Family involvement
10. Reflection
11. Contributions to the profession

Opportunity *for* **dialogue:**   Define these standards. What might they look like in a successful elementary classroom? How do they relate to the NCPTS?

NORTH CAROLINA STANDARD COURSE OF STUDY (NCSCS)

In addition to standards for teachers, each state has developed 21st Century standards for students. These standards answer the question: What should I teach? The North Carolina Standard Course of Study was first developed in 1898, but has been updated as recently as 2017. Accommodations are called for within the NCSCS for children with special needs, in accordance with their Individualized Education Plans. Standards are in place for each grade K-12, for the following subjects:

- English Language Arts
- Mathematics
- Science
- Social Studies
- Arts Education
- Guidance
- English as a Second Language
- Healthful Living
- Information and Technology Skills
- World Languages
- Career Technical Education

Most state standards are developed as a spiraling curriculum. This means that specific skills are repeated every year with the understanding that they will develop over time. For example, in the NCSCS, for English Language Arts, Anchor Standard 1 for literature reads, "Read closely to determine what the text says explicitly and to make logical inferences from it; cite specific textual evidence when writing or speaking to support conclusions from the text." For the same goal, a kindergartener is expected to answer questions about key details in a text with prompting and support, whereas a fifth-grader is expected to quote accurately from a text when explaining what the text says and when drawing inferences from the text. In Mathematics, in terms of "Measurement and Data," kindergarteners are expected to describe and compare measurable attributes of objects, whereas fourth graders should (for example) be able to compare those items by estimating and measuring with metric units.

Opportunity *for* **dialogue:** In what ways are the NC Professional Teaching Standards related to the implementation of the NC Standard Course of Study?

COMMON CORE

From 2012-2017 North Carolina used the Common Core standards. Although they are no longer used in North Carolina, they are still common in many states across the country. The Common Core State Standards are part of a national effort led by The National Governors Association for Best Practices and The Council of Chief State School Officers to make learning objectives consistent state-to-state. The Common Core State standards are intended to build on the strengths of current state standards, raise expectations, and take into account standards from top performing countries around the world with a goal of preparing students to compete globally. They are aligned with college and work expectations, and include accommodations for English Language Learners and Students with Disabilities.

The Common Core standards were also developed as a spiraling curriculum. For example, in the Reading Standards for Literature, one area of focus is on "Key Ideas and Details." For this area of focus, a kindergartener is expected to answer questions about key details in a text with prompting and support, whereas a second-grader is expected to ask and answer such questions as *who, what, where, when, why* and *how* to demonstrate understanding of key details. In Mathematics, one area of focus is on "Number and Operations in Base 10." For this area of focus, a kindergartener is expected to "work with numbers 11-19 to gain foundations for place value," whereas a second grader is expected to "use place value understanding and properties of operation to add and subtract. Place value in kindergarten is an example of raising standards; with the Common Core, mathematical skills are delivered to students on average two grades earlier. These standards are available in full detail at www.corestandards.org.

ELEMENTARY PROGRAMS AND PRACTICES
EDN 300
OPPORTUNITY FOR DIALOGUE

Name:

Chapter:

CHAPTER nine
Issues Facing Educators

Someone needs to do a study to determine the place of passion and love in learning.

– Mem Fox

CASE STUDY 1 – TEST LOCKDOWN

For 10 years, I taught elementary school in a low-income, predominantly African American community in Florida. In January, I visited this school. I had not visited the building in several years, and I immediately noticed there had been several changes since I left.

The school had not made Adequate Yearly Progress by No Child Left Behind standards for five consecutive years. The principal was under a lot of pressure from the state to show improvement in standardized test scores or face possible takeover by the state. The upper-elementary grades had adopted a district-imposed curriculum, requiring adherence to a minute-by-minute schedule the principal referred to as "explicit, systematic instruction." For example, the instruction included 20 daily minutes of word study from grade-leveled disposable index cards. This study was further divided into 4-minute specific word objectives that were taking place simultaneously in all fourth grade classrooms that I observed. The role of teachers had seemingly been reduced to following a script.

Speaking to the teachers, I was told how they were now required to spend time compiling lists of scores and charts, matching ultra-specific skills to standard numbers. Each fourth grade teacher was observed weekly by school administrators or district officials to make sure specific objective numbers could be found posted on the board. This day, each teacher's whiteboard read, "CBC 4.1.2A/SSS LA.A.2.2.1: identifying relevant supporting details/facts, essential message and arranging events in chronological order."

A former colleague of mine told me that her poetry unit (a favorite of her students while I was there) had been criticized by the administration for not being linked to state standards. She could not simply teach poetry to inspire interest and provoke enjoyment; she could only utilize a poem in order to meet state standards such as LA.A.2.2.1. Of course, linking lessons to state objectives is a normal practice throughout the country. However, it is the stipulation that teachers in low-performing schools must apply this practice to every miniscule segment of instruction that renders student interest and enjoyment irrelevant distractions. Speaking of which, the most distinct difference I noticed was with the students. They no longer seemed to be the fun-loving bunch I remembered. No one laughed, no one smiled. Even during the lunch period I attended, the lunch monitors had instituted "silent lunches" for the week.

Another thing I found out was that from January through the day of the state test in March, the school had instituted what the principal referred to as "Test Lockdown." For this period, during what used to be Art, Music, and Spanish classes, the students had an additional section of their Reading class in an attempt to improve students' "levels," or test scores.

As I was leaving, I spent time talking to a student I encountered in the hallway. "Where are you headed?" I asked him. "To test lockdown," he answered. "I'm a level 2."

ELEMENTARY PROGRAMS AND PRACTICES
EDN 300
CASE ANALYSIS

Name:

Case Study:

Problem (identify the primary problem faced by the student(s) and/or teacher(s)):

Facts (list the facts from the case that are relevant to solving the problem):

Questions (identify questions about the case you would like answered):

Topics for further research (based on the questions, identify some areas for further research):

*Be prepared to propose a potential solution to the problem based on your research and experience.

CASE STUDY 2 – CAN'T WE GET HIM SENT TO A SPECIAL CLASS?

Theresa is a young fourth year second grade teacher. She, like most elementary school teachers, is from a white middle-class background. Theresa has recently been transferred to a new school because of staff shortages. Her previous school was a middle-class school in a suburban neighborhood. Although there were some non-white students at the school, for four years Theresa had never taught one. Her new school is only 3 miles away from her previous school; however, the school population differs in that about 10% of the student-body comes from a public housing complex. These children are almost exclusively from low-income, single-parent households and are African American.

In her first year at the new school, it was evident that Theresa was having some trouble with one of her students. She told the assistant principal that Julian, one of three African American students in her classroom, and the only African American boy, was having learning and behavioral problems. Julian's standardized test scores were actually near the middle of the class academically. A brief observation of Theresa's classroom would make it clear that Julian is one of a group of four boys who liked to talk in class, sometimes out of turn, and played tag together on the playground. As a result of his behaviors and perceived learning difficulties, Theresa decided to write a referral to the school counselor in which she made the following statements:

- Julian does not care about school, he does not want to learn.

- His behavior is disrupting the class, he probably does not have a good role model in his family at home.

- His play on the playground is scary and intimidating.

Janet, the school counselor, has been at the school for 10 years and is well respected by her colleagues. As a result of the referral, Janet spent time talking to Julian one-on-one. She also spent time talking to Julian's mother by telephone. Among others, her notes included the following statements:

- Julian talked about how he loves coming to school, and that playground time is his favorite.

- Julian's mother assists with his homework every night.

- Julian's mother has had no contact with his teacher.

After her evaluation, which revealed no learning or behavioral problems, Janet walked Julian back to Theresa's classroom. Theresa looked at him sternly and directed him to "find a seat away from everyone else trying to do good work." She then turned to Janet and asked, "What is wrong with him, can't we get him sent to a special class?"

ELEMENTARY PROGRAMS AND PRACTICES
EDN 300
CASE ANALYSIS

Name:

Case Study:

Problem (identify the primary problem faced by the student(s) and/or teacher(s)):

Facts (list the facts from the case that are relevant to solving the problem):

Questions (identify questions about the case you would like answered):

Topics for further research (based on the questions, identify some areas for further research):

*Be prepared to propose a potential solution to the problem based on your research and experience.

CASE STUDY 3 – LOSING CONTROL

Mr. Lacey is a first year teacher.

During his internship, he taught in a second grade class with 16 students. He entered the class mid-semester, and his cooperating teacher was an excellent mentor. She had a clear teaching philosophy based largely on a John Dewey's philosophy of inquiry-based learning. Much of the day revolved around centers and small group work. Along with his cooperating teacher, Mr. Lacey, the teacher assistant, and a rotating volunteer created a 4:1 child-to-teacher ratio for the majority of the day. The behavior plan in classroom was clear; the students had to reflect on any negative behaviors in a "behavior journal" at the back table, which was signed by parents each week. The class was a well-oiled machine, however, and these incidents were infrequent. Mr. Lacey hoped to create a similar environment in his first classroom.

This year, Mr. Lacey found a job a week before the school year started. He was assigned to a fifth grade classroom in a larger neighboring district. His class list included 27 students, and the principal warned him that they often have a few more enrollees on the first day. Mr. Lacey began the year with his cooperating teacher's daily plan in place. Students worked in centers and small groups for the majority of the day. There was no teacher assistant or other help in the room, and Mr. Lacey was having trouble managing the small groups. It seemed as he focused on one group, the rest would be off-task. His back table "behavior journal" area soon became a double table that some students visited 9 or 10 times per day, some refusing to write a thing. Mr. Lacey felt as if he was losing control.

He continued with centers because he knew that small groups were optimal learning environments for children, however, he began to doubt whether his class was learning at all. Whereas some spent the majority of their day journaling about their bad behavior, others breezed through the centers and sat idly while waiting to move to the next group. Mr. Lacey noticed, but often ignored this as he was working closely with one small-group at a time.

By week four, Mr. Lacey was exasperated and considering change.

ELEMENTARY PROGRAMS AND PRACTICES
EDN 300
CASE ANALYSIS

Name:

Case Study:

Problem (identify the primary problem faced by the student(s) and/or teacher(s)):

Facts (list the facts from the case that are relevant to solving the problem):

Questions (identify questions about the case you would like answered):

Topics for further research (based on the questions, identify some areas for further research):

*Be prepared to propose a potential solution to the problem based on your research and experience.

CASE STUDY 4 – TEACHER'S LOUNGE

Ms. Pelaez, a first year fourth grade teacher, enters the teachers' lounge during her lunch period on Friday of the first week of school. Mrs. Cook and Ms. Pennyfeather, two veteran teachers, are already in the lounge having lunch.

Mrs. Cook: Hi Ms. Pelaez, how has your first week been?

Ms. Pelaez: So far, so good. Thanks for asking.

Ms. Pennyfeather: "So far" is right, wait until those kids get comfortable. Then they will show their true colors.

Ms. Pelaez: I am sure they will be okay.

Mrs. Cook: Don't let your guard down Ms. Pelaez. These kids are terrible! Don't you have Justin Adams?

Ms. Pelaez: Yes, he seems so smart!

Mrs. Cook: Oh boy, I had him last year. He is impossible. He did not listen to a thing. I spent half my year yelling at him to flip his cards, and I had to call his mother every week... and his mother acted as if she didn't even care!

Ms. Pelaez: Really? I called his mother this week to introduce myself, and she was very receptive. In fact, she was one of the parents most interested in the classroom routine.

Ms. Pennyfeather: You'll learn, Ms. Pelaez. Those kids will be off the wall by next week. Just make sure they have their test books open when Principal Daniels walks in, that's what I do; and as long as I am practicing for that test, she doesn't bother with me.

Ms. Pelaez: Sounds boring for the kids.

Ms. Pennyfeather: They'll live. All they do is act up anyway.

Mrs. Cook: Oh, and you have Wanda Johnston, too!? Boy, are you in for it!

Ms. Pelaez: Why is that?

Mrs. Cook: Well, that child just refuses to learn. Flat out refuses! She could not catch up to third grade reading, and I had her for two years. Like I have time to slow it down for her!

Ms. Pelaez: Sounds like you had a tough year last year.

Mrs. Cook: Every year is a struggle. I am counting the days to retirement.

ELEMENTARY PROGRAMS AND PRACTICES
EDN 300
CASE ANALYSIS

Name:

Case Study:

Problem (identify the primary problem faced by the student(s) and/or teacher(s)):

Facts (list the facts from the case that are relevant to solving the problem):

Questions (identify questions about the case you would like answered):

Topics for further research (based on the questions, identify some areas for further research):

*Be prepared to propose a potential solution to the problem based on your research and experience.

CASE STUDY 5 – ASSESSING, ASSESSING, ASSESSING

Dale is a veteran teacher of 19 years. He is teaching fourth grade in a suburban elementary school. He has seen a lot of change during his time as a teacher. Currently, his principal and the associate superintendent over elementary schools in his school district have encouraged teachers to make data-based decisions in their classrooms. They are being asked to make sure that every curricular decision is based on research and information they have about the students. In an effort to better know students, the district has purchased hand-held, electronic devices for teachers to use in their assessment of reading. Each teacher, including Dale, received 10 hours of inservice training to help them be proficient in doing the assessments. Now, every two weeks, Dale is required to do an assessment for each child. One of the assessments is like a Running Record, during which a child reads a passage and Dale records when a mistake is made. The computer automatically figures the percentages and creates a report showing what grade level the student is on. Another assessment is a fluency check. Students are asked to read passages as quickly as possible and Dale records the number of words they are able to read in one minute. A chart is kept for each child with goals for improvement.

Dale is frustrated with this. The assessment is taking so much time, he has asked for assistants to come and help. He asked his principal if there was someone who could come and watch his class while he takes students to a quiet area to do the testing. Dale was in the teacher's lounge and overheard the following conversation. These two teachers were fourth grade teachers in the school as well.

Bonnie: Well, I finally finished my fluency testing. I just don't understand why we have to do this stuff. It takes up so much time. I don't know what it means, either. Scott is one of my best readers when it comes to comprehension and the amount of reading he does at home, but he cannot meet his goal for fluency.

Jim: Just last week, Zalore's mother came to talk to me about the report we sent home. She said she can't believe that Zalore is below grade level and is receiving low grades. She said that Zalore is reading a sixth grade novel at home and comprehends it perfectly. I don't understand what this testing is all about. It seems like we don't have time to teach because we are spending so much time testing.

The next day, Dale was in his room when Michael came into the room with excitement on his face. He actually started talking before he came into the room. "Mr. Osborn, look what I got. It's a garden spider and it built a giant web in our tomato garden. Can we keep it in the room? Can we learn about spiders today? Do you know how it makes its web? What does it eat?"

Dale cringed as he had to say, "Mike, yes, it would be fun to keep the spider in our room. Let's do that. But, we won't have time to learn about spiders today. It's your turn for your fluency test and then we have to do a running record."

Dale was heart-broken when he saw the look of complete disappointment in Mike's face.

ELEMENTARY PROGRAMS AND PRACTICES
EDN 300
CASE ANALYSIS

Name:

Case Study:

Problem (identify the primary problem faced by the student(s) and/or teacher(s)):

Facts (list the facts from the case that are relevant to solving the problem):

Questions (identify questions about the case you would like answered):

Topics for further research (based on the questions, identify some areas for further research):

*Be prepared to propose a potential solution to the problem based on your research and experience.

CASE STUDY 6 – A SAMPLE OF QUESTIONS HEARD IN CLASSROOMS

As we listen to the kinds of questions being asked in a classroom by teachers and students, we can get a good indication of the kind of classroom we are in. Here are some examples:

From students:
Teacher, I'm done. What do I do now?

Could you go over that again, I don't understand how it works?

What will we get if we do that assignment?

Here is how I did it, what do you think?

This is boring, when can we go outside?

Is there a really good book you think I would like?

I don't know.

I did my homework last night and checked the answers. I don't know why I got this one wrong. Can you help me?

Can I go to the bathroom?

From teachers:
How many sentences are there in a paragraph?

Can you draw a diagram or a picture representing a significant thing you learned today from the story we are reading?

Can you draw a picture of your favorite part of the story?

Did Thomas Jefferson write the Declaration of Independence?

How do you think Thomas Jefferson felt as he shared the Declaration of Independence with others who were working with him?

What is the best part of the piece you have just written?

Can you tell me the main characters of the story?

Please share how you are feeling about the main character in this story.

Can you please explain why that works?

Is this the correct answer?

What do you think would help you learn this the best?

What part of this would you like to learn more about?

What do you think? What don't you understand?

Can you explain why this works when we do it this way?

ELEMENTARY PROGRAMS AND PRACTICES
EDN 300
CASE ANALYSIS

Name:

Case Study:

Problem (is there a problem with some of these questions?):

Facts (identify which questions are problematic and why):

Questions (identify questions about the case you would like answered):

Topics for further research (based on the questions, identify some areas for further research):

*Be prepared to propose a potential solution to the problem based on your research and experience.

CASE STUDY 7 – AN EXCITING ELEMENTARY SCHOOL

Greg Maughan, a fifth grade teacher at Sage Creek Elementary School, was putting the last of his materials away for the year. He had just completed his first year teaching. As he did so, he began to think about his first year. He felt like he had had a wonderful experience. He knew he was fortunate to be hired in a dynamic school. He remembered so many positive things that had happened in the school. Here are some of them:

The school had worked with the local Kiwanis club and arranged to have retired members and their spouses come to the school every day to read to or with the students. They called them their foster grandparents. The kids just loved them. He remembered watching Reddick sit down next to one of the "grandpas," reading and discussing a book that Reddick would not have been able to read alone.

Several fathers of students at the school brought their snowmobiles to the school one day during the winter. The children, parents, teachers, and administrators had spent that day playing in the snow. They had snowmobile rides, built snowmen, had snowball fights, played fox and geese (a game of tag in the snow), and enjoyed a day together outside. At the end of the day, they went inside and had hot chocolate and donuts. They sat around and talked and talked. The next day, Greg discovered that things were different. The students seemed a little more interested in sharing and in asking questions. He felt like their relationship had been strengthened. The classroom was different and it was better.

His mind went back to the special day in the fall when they had taken every student in the school to the state fair. The bus ride to the fair was about an hour. But he remembered how excited the students were and how much they all enjoyed that day.

In February, the principal had taken the entire faculty to the state math conference. Greg remembered how he had enjoyed that time to learn with his colleagues and talk about ways to improve their math program at the school. He thought about how faculty meetings were focused on learning about more effective ways to teach and assess. The principal would send all of the announcements via email so that they had time to talk about significant issues of learning and teaching.

Next, Greg thought about the checker, chess, carom, and crokinole tournaments the teachers had sponsored; inviting children to play before school, during recesses, and after school. That was another activity that had helped to create excitement in the school.

He remembered Ms. Puckett telling the fifth grades, "Give me a seed and I'll help you grow it." He had learned so much about how to really help students grow as writers, as he had watched Ms. Puckett do writing conferences with her students and how she had organized so everyone could share and learn from each other. He remembered what a difference Ms. Puckett's idea of setting aside 45 minutes each day for personal exploration had made. Their students would come to school excited to explore aspects of the world in which they were excited. He marveled at the passion for learning he saw in these fifth graders.

As Greg closed the lock on his cabinet, he smiled to himself. He had had a great year. He was so excited to be able to do it again, starting in August. He hoped it would be a short summer.

ELEMENTARY PROGRAMS AND PRACTICES
EDN 300
CASE ANALYSIS

Name:

Case Study:

Problem:

Why is this not the case at all elementary schools?

Facts (list the facts from the case that are relevant to solving the problem):

Questions (identify questions about the case you would like answered):

Topics for further research (based on the questions, identify some areas for further research):

***Be prepared to propose a potential solution to the problem based on your research and experience.**

CASE STUDY 8 – CONVERSATION WITH A COLLEAGUE

I just hung up the phone on a wonderful conversation with Pam, a colleague with whom I have worked for years. She is an elementary school teacher with exceptional abilities. I always like going to her classroom. Her passion for teaching, the level of caring for her students, and her commitment and dedication to students are incredible. She is a good example of the powerful impact teachers can have on their students. I have always been impressed with the growth that her students make and the excitement they have for learning. It was good to talk with her. However, I detected a sense of sadness in her voice.

Pam took a leave of absence from her school and moved out of state to help a family member with some health issues. After a while, she took the opportunity to work as a substitute in some of the local schools in the area. During our conversation, Pam expressed her concern about the schools in which she was subbing.

She asked, "When you think about education in this state that I am in, what do you usually think about?"

I replied, "My first thought is of Dr. So-and So, and Ms. So-and So, who are wonderful educators and have done so much to help us understand how to best support children as they learn. I guess I would also picture effective schools doing the exciting things these educators taught."

Pam responded, "That's what I thought, too, but that is not what I am finding. On the first day I was asked to sub, I took a bag full of good children's books with me. I knew that all children enjoy being read to and we would enjoy good books in between the assignments that had been outlined for the students. I was looking forward to working with children again. You can imagine my shock when I got to the school and the other teachers and the principal told me that they didn't have time to read aloud to children. They said that they had too much other work to do and asked me not to read aloud to the students."

She went on, "When I got to the classroom, I saw a pile of worksheets that had been prepared. I found out that I was expected to have the students complete the worksheets that had been prepared for them. Each worksheet focused on one aspect of the upcoming tests. I was shocked to also discover that my whole class never met together in my classroom after the morning announcements. I didn't see my whole class together for the rest of the day. The students had been assigned to a variety of groups according to their needs. Each group had a specific worksheet focused on the skill with which they needed practice. The groups lasted for about 20 or 30 minutes and then they would go to the next group. By the end of the day, I was exhausted. I realized that I had not had any fun that day. I certainly wasn't excited to go back the next day.

"Later, I learned that there was an opening for a teacher in that school beginning in the fall. I thought it over and decided I wanted to get back into the classroom but I would apply at a different school."

ELEMENTARY PROGRAMS AND PRACTICES
EDN 300
CASE ANALYSIS

Name:

Case Study:

Problem (identify the primary problem faced by the student(s) and/or teacher(s)):

Facts (list the facts from the case that are relevant to solving the problem):

Questions (identify questions about the case you would like answered):

Topics for further research (based on the questions, identify some areas for further research):

*Be prepared to propose a potential solution to the problem based on your research and experience.

Case Study 9 – An ESL story

Ms. Johnson is a first year 5th grade teacher at Watson Elementary. Mrs. Hernandez, her teaching assistant, has been at the school for seven years, and was a teacher in Mexico before moving to the United States. Their class has 20 students, and nine are labeled ESL. Of those nine, there are three from Mexico, two from Guatemala, two from Puerto Rico, and two cousins from Haiti who arrived in the country mid school-year. The other 11 students are English-speaking and White. The only two Latino students with any knowledge of English are the two girls from Puerto Rico, who speak Spanish at home, but English in the classroom. The two Haitian students have a working knowledge of English, but they prefer to speak to each other in Haitian-Creole.

Ms. Hunter, the principal, is very concerned with both the academic performance and behavior of the students in Ms. Johnson's class. The students are making academic gains at a slower rate than the other classrooms, and many of the ESL students are not making progress with their English. Ms. Hunter says that when Ms. Johnson is leading the class the students seem rowdy, and are free to get out of their seats. She only sees the class quiet during Mrs. Hernandez's morning meeting. Also, there are some other specific things that are troubling her: The students from Puerto Rico often make derogatory remarks to the Mexican and Guatemalan students, calling them "reffies" (short for refugee and meant as an insult for their lack of English). The Haitian students are largely ignored; they are the only Black students in the school, and at this point have made no other friends. The Hispanic and White girls seem to get along, but the boys are very competitive. They play soccer every day at recess on teams split by race, and games often escalate to the point where they come inside glaring at each other.

In the classroom Ms. Johnson and Mrs. Hernandez do not see eye-to-eye. In terms of pedagogy, Ms. Johnson was trained as an ESL teacher. One of the major focuses at her university was authentic interaction in English. Her teaching style focuses on presenting everything, including vocabulary words and specific information in the most natural context possible. Mrs. Hernandez, on the other hand, believes that the ESL students need to be told what to do in their native language otherwise they will not be able to obey. She thinks having a "natural" conversation in English is for naught, when many of the ESL students cannot understand one word Ms. Johnson is saying, and that the English speakers are bored by these conversations and not paying attention and misbehaving. When it comes to behavior management, Ms. Johnson wants her students to feel a sense of autonomy, and is not bothered by students moving around the classroom. Also, she I focused on developing positive mentoring relationships with her students. She has focused these efforts particularly on the ESL students since several have had a terrible time leaving their home countries, and have been separated from their parents. She is aware that some are angry and upset with circumstances which have separated them from their families and have brought them to a foreign country to learn. Ms. Hernandez, on the other hand, spends at least 20 minutes each morning delivering a stern moral lecture to the students, in English and Spanish. The students are completely silent during this time. She feels that children need moral guidance as much as they need a good formal education. She teaches them to stay in their seats and respect authority, and sometimes tests vocabulary with flashcards.

Ms. Hunter is considering some changes for the following school year.

ELEMENTARY PROGRAMS AND PRACTICES
EDN 300
CASE ANALYSIS

Name:

Case Study:

Problem (identify the primary problem faced by the student(s) and/or teacher(s)):

Facts (list the facts from the case that are relevant to solving the problem):

Questions (identify questions about the case you would like answered):

Topics for further research (based on the questions, identify some areas for further research):

*Be prepared to propose a potential solution to the problem based on your research and experience.

CASE STUDY 10 – TEACHER BURNOUT

Ms. Nishimoto was sitting at her desk at the end of a long day. She felt good about what she and her 2nd grade students had accomplished. After the students had gone home and she had met with the parents of one of her students, she quickly met with other teachers in her school that were serving on the school improvement team she chaired. After that meeting, she had returned to her room, responded to the learning logs the students had turned in, checked over the math test they had taken that afternoon, fine-tuned her lesson plans, and made sure that all materials were ready for the next day. She took just a minute to tidy up the room and make sure the book center looked inviting and showcased the new books she had added to their classroom library. She was tired, but she was happy. This was her 10th year teaching. She knew that her students were making good progress. The reading conferences she had had with her students this week were especially productive. They were happy. They were excited about the social studies projects they were doing and the class book they had just written about their trip to the a local farm. She sat back down at her desk and wrote notes to five of her students whom she wanted to compliment for various things she had observed them doing.

She was just about ready to leave for home when her across the hall colleague, Freda Sanchez came into her room and hesitantly asked if Ms. Nishimoto had a few minutes to talk. Ms. Sanchez was in her third year of teaching. Ms. Nishimoto had noticed that for the past three weeks, Ms. Sanchez looked tired and unhappy. She seemed more on edge and had less patience with her students. Ms. Nishimoto had also noticed that Ms. Sanchez's children seemed less happy than they had at the first of the year. There were more classroom management issues in that classroom than there had been earlier in the year.

As Ms. Sanchez sat down, she started to unload. She said that she was really struggling. She didn't see how she could go on. She explained how she wasn't happy and didn't find joy in teaching like she had when she started. She talked about how her students seemed bored and weren't willing to work. She thought her lessons were bland and lacked the spark needed to help her students engage and be excited about learning. Ms. Sanchez described how she couldn't see that she was making a difference in any of her students and how she hated having to use the district mandated curricula and assessment. She pointed to her bag filled with papers to grade and complained that she spent hours every night grading worksheets. She didn't have time to do anything but school stuff. She took some time to articulate a list of all the things her students couldn't do or weren't doing well. It was apparent to Ms. Nishimoto that her colleague was, indeed, frustrated and discouraged.

Ms. Sanchez finally said, "I guess I'm just burned out. I'm not sure I even want to be a teacher." After a short pause, she turned to Ms. Nishimoto and said, "You always seem so happy. I can see that your students are happy and excited to learn. What should I do? Can you help me?"

Elementary Programs and Practices
EDN 300
Case Analysis

Name:

Case Study:

Problem (identify the primary problem faced by the student(s) and/or teacher(s)):

Facts (list the facts from the case that are relevant to solving the problem):

Questions (identify questions about the case you would like answered):

Topics for further research (based on the questions, identify some areas for further research):

*Be prepared to propose a potential solution to the problem based on your research and experience.

REFERENCES

Chapter 1: What is our work? What Should it Be?

Allington, Richard L. "The Schools We Have. The Schools We Need." *Reading Teacher*, Sep 94, v. 48 i. 1, 14-29.

Touchstone Pictures, *Dead Poet's Society*, (1989).

Chapter 2: Philosophical Foundations

Cambourne, B. (1988). *The Whole Story: Natural learning and the acquisition of literacy in the classroom.* Auckland, New Zealand: Ashton Scholastic, Ltd.

Harste, J., Short, K., & Burke, C. (1995). *Creating Classrooms for Authors and Inquirers.* Portsmouth, NH: Heinemann.

Mandel, B. J., (Ed). (1980). *Three Language-Arts Curriculum Models: Pre-Kindergarten through College.* Urbana, Illinois: National Council of Teachers of English.

Speare, E. B. (1961). *The bronze bow.* New York: Houghton Mifflin.

Walker, B.L. (2007). "Balanced Literacy for Diverse Learners" in B. Honchell & M. Schulz (Eds) *Literacy for Diverse Learners: Finding Common Ground in Today's Classrooms,* 67-108. Norwood, Massachusetts: Christopher Gordon Publishers, Inc.

Chapter 4: Classroom Management

Clark, R. (2003). *The Essential 55.* New York: Hyperion.

Chapter 5: Diversity

Delpit, L. (2006). "Lessons from teachers." *Journal of Teacher Education, 57*(3), 220-231.

Ladson-Billings, G. (1995). Toward a theory of culturally relevant pedagogy. *American Educational Research Journal, 32*(3), 465-491.

McKown, C., & Weinstein, R. S. (2003). The development and consequences of stereotype consciousness in middle childhood. *Child Development, 74*(2), 498-515.

Wasserberg, M. J. (2014). Stereotype threat effects on African American children in an urban elementary school. *The Journal of Experimental Education, 82*(4), 502-517.

Chapter 8: Teaching Standards

North Carolina Professional Teaching Standards Commission. (2007). *North Carolina Professional Teaching Standards.* Retrieved from http://www.ncptsc.org/StandardsDocs/Final%20Standards%20Document.pdf

National Board for Professional Teaching Standards. (2002). *The Five Core Propo-sitions.* Retrieved from http://www.nbpts.org/the_standards/the_five_core_propositio

National Board for Professional Teaching Standards. (2001). *NBPTS Early Child-hood Generalist Standards: Second Edition.* Retrieved from http://www.nbpts.org/userfiles/File/ec_gen_standards.pdf

National Board for Professional Teaching Standards. (2001). *NBPTS Middle Child-hood Generalist Standards: Second Edition.* Retrieved from http://www.nbpts.org/userfiles/File/mc_gen_standards.pdf

CPSIA information can be obtained
at www.ICGtesting.com
Printed in the USA
LVHW012002301219
642080LV00002B/2/P

9 781524 989750